EGA/VGA
A Programmer's
Reference Guide

EGA/VGA
A Programmer's
Reference Guide

89'

Bradley Dyck Kliewer

Bradley Dyck Kliewer '85
1/19/88

Intertext Publications
McGraw-Hill Book Company
New York, N.Y.

Library of Congress Catalog Card Number 87-831 02

10 9 8 7 6 5 4 3 2 1

ISBN 0-07-035089-2

Intertext Publications/Multiscience Press, Inc.
McGraw-Hill Book Company
11 West 19th Street
New York, NY 10011

Composed in Ventura Publisher by Context, Inc.

Contents

To my wife, Sue,
and our parents,
Henry and Rosella Kliewer
and
C. J. and Wilma Dyck
You've been a source of inspiration and support

Preface

Since its introduction in late 1984, the Enhanced Graphics Adapter (EGA) has become the graphics standard in the IBM Personal Computer world. Now, with the introduction of the Video Graphics Array (VGA), the EGA is joined by a new, more sophisticated and complex graphics standard. Because the EGA is the most popular add-on board for the millions of PCs, XTs, ATs, and clones in use, and the VGA is the standard for the new PS/2 series of 80286 and 80386 computers, it is clear that anyone interested in programming or taking full advantage of graphics for these machines had better know all of the ins and outs of these graphics standards.

However, getting beneath the surface of these two boards is not so easy. Documentation for the EGA and VGA is scattered among separate manuals, densely written and difficult to understand, and often sketchy. Moreover, the manuals give very few examples of code, and many of those given are only fragments which must be combined with your own routines to create a working example. And, while there are good magazine articles about EGA/VGA programming, it is certainly difficult to reference dozens of these articles to locate a desired explanation, and it is also difficult to coordinate the terminology which varies somewhat from article to article.

So, in addition to the challenge of programming these sophisticated boards, it has been the programmer's burden to have to piece together the available information to gain a working understanding of the graphics adapters.

The goal of *EGA/VGA A Programmer's Reference Guide* is to correct this difficult situation by collecting in one volume all of the scattered information about the EGA/VGA, as well as presenting a broad range of working programming examples and offering practical guidelines for effective and sophisticated EGA/VGA programming techniques.

EGA/VGA A Programmer's Reference Guide mixes reference materials and explanation with consistent and correct use of terminology in a manner which will add to the understanding of display programming, increase productivity, and enhance the craft and professionalism of the reader's programs.

In achieving these goals, what will be our priorities?

First, while several factors create an effective display, including speed, smoothness (freedom from flicker and other annoying effects), and layout, our focus will be on speed and smoothness: they are, after all, the easiest to quantify and the most technically difficult to achieve.

You have probably seen (or written) many games which flicker as the shapes are drawn, or seen entry areas on forms which flicker as the computer waits for user input. Flicker such as this is a common problem when programming with high-level languages. But if you look at commercial software, whether games or applications, the display remains rock steady. Professional programmers know how to coordinate video output with the adapter and display's internal timings. Usually, such programming is done with assembly language because it provides greater control over the hardware: determining the current status, and making direct changes. This book will teach you these assembly language techniques, so that you may apply them to your programs.

While we will concentrate on assembly language programming, the methods presented may be adapted to other languages if you know how to directly access memory, the I/O registers, and software interrupt routines. Although hardware control features are not typically a standard part of the language, many PC-based products add them (for example BASIC's PEEK, POKE, IN, and OUT, or Turbo Pascal's INTR, absolute memory functions, and ability to use inline code). We will begin with an introduction to BIOS programming — the simplest way to start programming. If you are an experienced assembly language programmer, you are probably familiar with BIOS programming and may want to skip ahead, using the BIOS call descriptions as reference material. For those of you fairly new to assembly language programming, you will quickly find that BIOS display writing routines are very slow and simply not adequate for most finished products. So, after finishing the BIOS routines, we will quickly move into register programming and much more sophisticated concepts.

You will find several small programs, which may seem rather dull compared with demonstration programs you may have seen. The aim is not to give dazzling demonstrations of the EGA/VGA's capabilities (you are probably already aware of such functions and want to create them for yourself), but rather to give simple, self-contained examples of the adapters' capabilities. Short programs are easier to enter without critical and frustrating mistakes. We want to encourage you to try the demonstrations, make your own modifications, and use them as a framework for your creative work. If you want to avoid entering the code, a source code diskette is available for an additional cost (see the order form at the back of the book).

If you are fairly new to assembly language programming, keep your eyes open! There are many useful tricks among the programming examples that go beyond graphics programming practices. For example, the ellipse program uses 32-bit and 48-bit integer arithmetic. It is really fairly simple and straightforward, yet it is a topic which is not often discussed (and the limits of 16-bit integers are often too constraining for many applications). You will also find practical uses for most of the 8088 assembly language instructions.

The example code may not always use the fastest or most elegant methods; I have tried to balance easy readability with considerations of speed and technique. I have also varied some methods from program to program as subtle examples of the many possible methods for achieving any particular function. The prime exceptions to this simplicity rule are the line and ellipse drawing programs. These programs have been tailored for speed and flexibility at the sacrifice of readability and code size.

Several of the BIOS programming examples will interact with each other. For example, the demonstration program for setting the mode places the adapter in 640 x 350 graphics mode, and does not switch back to the original mode at termination. You can then see the effect of several of the other BIOS routines while in graphics mode (typing MODE CO80 will return the display to alphanumeric mode). Several of the interactions are noted, and you can try these (and others) to better understand how BIOS functions.

Challenge yourself to improve the code. Where can you make it faster or more flexible? Does it need more range checking (or maybe less)? Watch for some of the tricks thrown into the code. Some standard methods for improving efficiency are using SUB or XOR to 0 a register (in place of MOV), or using shifts for division or multiplication by powers of two. But how about other constants? The MUL instruction is very slow; sometimes a sequence of ADD's and SHL's can be much faster (at the loss of flexibility since you cannot multiply by a variable).

If you do not have a list of instruction timings, you should get one. The Microsoft Macro Assembler comes with timing information, but there are other sources. Several books on assembly language programming, or the Intel *Programmer's Pocket Reference Guide* would be excellent supplemental material. If you really want to make your code efficient, you must consider several methods and decide which is the quickest. You can always use trial and error by timing each method, but frequently a quick glance at timings will immediately eliminate some methods. However, do not put too much faith in the timings; there will always be some variation due to the state of the prefetch cue, the actual processor used, and wait states on memory or port accesses (especially when dealing with display memory).

If efficiency is important you should time any routines which use roughly the same number of clock cycles. Try the code on different processors if possible, and loop through the code enough times to get several seconds of delay. Experimenting with different methods will make your code efficient and greatly improve your knowledge of the system. If you don't think efficiency is important, consider the amount of memory addressed by the EGA: 256K versus 16K on a color CGA screen. You won't usually update all of the memory, but simple images use more memory as the resolution and number of colors increase.

In addition to trying various instruction sequences, look for entirely different programming methods. The EGA and VGA provide many varied functions which can create similar effects. You will find four different ways to write to memory (along with many ways to modify the data as it is written). Study the registers (especially the Graphic Controller registers), and learn what they do. You may find functions you did not consider. Even if you do not have an application for a register, ask "what could this do for me?" A thorough understanding of the adapter's functions will improve your programming techniques, and the end result will be a better program.

Notes on Conventions Used

Hexadecimal numbers will be followed by a lowercase h; thus, 16 would be written as 10h in hexadecimal. Likewise, binary numbers will be followed by a lowercase b. Register names will be uppercase.

Medium resolution graphics will refer to 320 x 200 pixels; high resolution, 640 x 200; and enhanced 640 x 350. The VGA's new 640 x 480 mode will simply be called 640 x 480.

Adapters will be called the MDA (the original Monochrome Display Adapter), CGA (the original Color Graphics Adapter), EGA (Enhanced Graphics Adapter), and VGA (Video Graphics Array).

All references to DOS will assume version 2.0 or later, unless otherwise noted. All assembly language programs were assembled with Microsoft Macro Assembler version 4.0.

Compatibility modes will refer exclusively to graphics modes, since all alphanumeric modes are compatible between adapters.

The EGA and VGA have several methods of mapping memory into the PC's address space. The appearance of memory in this address space will be noted as the "CPU" or "processor" address; that is, where the 8088 or 8086 processor reads and writes the display.

1

The Question of Compatibility

The limitations of IBM's original Color Graphics Adapter (CGA) became apparent as graphics became increasingly important to business in the PC environment. The CGA was designed for compatibility with television sets and composite monitors, which were both cheap and prevalent. This limited the vertical resolution to 200 distinguishable lines. Horizontal resolution was designed for 320 rows, although 640 rows were possible on RGB and composite monitors.

Memory was expensive, and the creation of a reasonably priced color adapter required a limitation on available memory. The CGA was given enough memory (16K) for four colors with 320 x 200 resolution (the resolution which worked best on TV sets). Unfortunately, 16K is not enough memory for more than two colors in the 640 x 200 resolution mode, and one color has to be black. Even the four-color mode limits the user to only two sets of four colors, although the background can be changed in either set.

When the price of memory chips and other computer components began to fall and microcomputers started to replace larger systems, users complained about the poor selection of colors that could be used with the CGA. Viewing the 320 x 200 resolution for long periods of time was hard on eyes, and many graphics systems had to have a second monochrome monitor (with 720 x 350 nongraphics resolution) for working with text. In response, several companies developed boards for higher resolution graphics; many could use 16 or more colors. Hercules Computer Technologies produced the Hercules Card, which uses the higher resolution monochrome monitor for monochrome graphics.

Downward Compatibility

The greatest problem among the early high resolution graphics cards was a lack of standards or support of the CGA modes. Additionally, the programming methods used for many of these cards are inconsistent with the methods used by the CGA. The EGA addresses these issues by remaining very compatible with the CGA, extending available memory, and adding BIOS support for higher resolution. But the EGA standard is not without problems of its own. The large number of registers and operational modes make programming difficult unless you rely entirely on the slow BIOS routines. Most of the registers are write only; determining the current state of the adapter is almost impossible. This hinders the development of multi-tasking systems and memory resident programs, which need to save the video state before switching tasks. Like the Hercules card, an EGA with a monochrome display does not support CGA-compatible graphics.

In April 1987, IBM announced the PS/2 line of microcomputers. These computers included the new graphics device called the VGA (for Video Graphics Array, which refers to the single chip used by the system). The VGA is very similar to the EGA. It extends a few EGA functions and adds some higher resolution modes and a 256-color low resolution mode. Perhaps the most significant change for programmers, however, is the use of read/write registers. The VGA also uses analog displays rather than the digital type used by the EGA. As with the EGA, the VGA continues to support the original monochrome and CGA modes. Furthermore, all modes are supported by both the color and monochrome monitors.

The extent of EGA/CGA compatibility can be seen in the EGA's handling of the video BIOS routines located at INT 10h. The original BIOS routines are relocated to INT 42h and the EGA places its own BIOS code at INT 10h. The EGA BIOS calls the old routines for some functions, so the EGA is truly a BIOS extension rather than a replacement of the original BIOS functions. The original BIOS calls are fully supported, and the operation of the new calls remains consistent with the old.

Although BIOS calls remain compatible between the various IBM (and compatible) adapters, there are a few differences among the common hardware interface ports. The monochrome/CGA and EGA/VGA architectures are quite different. The original adapters are based on the Motorola 6845 graphics controller, while the EGA and VGA use proprietary IBM chips (of course, a number of manufacturers have developed chip sets which are nearly identical). Several of the EGA and VGA registers mimic the behavior of the 6845; those that are different are noted in the chapters on register programming.

Despite some of the differences among the various adapters (which deal primarily with the type of display used), IBM includes a great deal of support for CGA and MDA emulation which is buried amongst the many features and functions. For example, the EGA monochrome alphanumeric mode modifies the character set very slightly to exactly match the MDA. And, while the VGA usually double scans CGA graphics modes (to generate 400 lines, addressable as 200 lines), it is possible to switch to a true 200 line display.

Flexibility (Pages of Memory, Alternate Character Sets, Monitors)

The EGA works with the original color and monochrome displays. It also provides support for the ECD (Enhanced Color Display), which has nearly the same resolution as the monochrome monitor (640 x 350 for the ECD versus 720 x 350 for the monochrome adapter), and 16 colors out of a possible 64. The adapter can change any one of the 16 colors to any of the other 63. The VGA does not support any of the original displays (although some multisynch displays can be adapted). Instead, the VGA requires an analog display. The VGA's highest resolution mode is 640 x 480 and may use 16 colors (or shades of gray) out of a possible 262,144 (64 shades of gray). As with the EGA, the VGA colors are fully selectable.

IBM also provides for memory expansion on the EGA so that two separate pages of high resolution color graphics are possible. EGA compatibles come with a full complement of memory, as does the VGA. With lower resolution (or monochrome graphics), up to eight pages of text or graphics can be stored on the adapter. It is possible to display one page while another is being modified and alternately display several pages. The extra memory can also be used for storing font tables (although this is not possible in graphics mode), and have up to 1024 different characters (2048 on the VGA), 512 of which can be displayed at any one time.

The ability to modify fonts, work with additional characters, and individually select colors only hints at the power and flexibility provided on the EGA and VGA. Almost any display attribute can be modified. Characters can be made larger or smaller than the standard sizes, and the number of lines displayed on the screen can be changed. Changes may be made on a temporary basis (only within a particular application) or on a more permanent basis (affecting all programs until the system is rebooted or reprogrammed). Programming advanced graphics applications in this type of environment requires a much more relativistic approach than the CGA.

Perhaps the most noticeable architectural change is the organization of EGA/VGA memory. The CGA uses sequential data bits to describe each color pixel. While this method is fairly easy to program, it wastes processor address space (doubling the number of colors doubles the size of the memory map) and significantly slows graphics applications that use many colors (doubling the number of colors tends to double the time it takes to write memory). The EGA and VGA use a bit plane technique, which "stacks" the color bits at the same address. Bit planes allow more color combinations to be added without increasing processor address space. In some cases, bit plane architecture can speed writing memory, since one write can modify eight bits in each plane. The details of these various modes are discussed in the following chapters.

So, we have traced the development of graphics adapter standards and hinted at the new features and flexibility available, but what does the future hold? The VGA is beginning to push the current processors to their limits. The maximum memory segment size of 64K is nearly filled by the 256-color mode, and handling the 640 x 480 display slows even the fastest processors (especially since the adapter must also address this memory, and locks out the processor by inserting wait states). The next step will probably be to more sophisticated graphics coprocessors which allow simultaneous access, and built-in graphics primitives such as line and circle drawing.

It is difficult to predict whether these new adapters will remain backwards compatible with the EGA/VGA standard. However, the EGA/VGA standard will be around for years to come. The coprocessor-based adapters are quite expensive (and so are the high resolution displays), and even as they drop in price, the EGA/VGA technology will get cheaper as well. For most people, the EGA is sufficient for most any application.

Games are very impressive on the EGA with its enhanced resolution and 16 colors. Even as the simple 8086/8088 has dominated the home market for years, you can expect the same for the EGA and VGA. Business graphics and presentations look brilliant and sharp in 16 colors at enhanced resolutions. By convention, standard business graphs have no more than 4 colors (plus black and white) and the EGA's selection of 64 is adequate. The business market, which is the driving force behind IBM's marketing, does not need significant improvements in graphics technology.

The main areas which would benefit from faster, higher resolution graphics are sophisticated desktop publishing systems, graphics window-based programs, and Computer Aided Design. Applications which work with digitized color images would also benefit from increased resolution and color support, although the VGA's 256-color mode can reproduce some very realistic images despite its low resolution.

So, programs you develop for the EGA or VGA should remain marketable for several years. However, if you want to stay prepared for the next generation of displays and operating systems, you should write modular code.

2

Introduction to BIOS
Writing Modifiable Programs

When writing complicated applications, you should consider future upgrades to your program, including new features and support for new hardware or operating systems. Programming with BIOS routines has often been suggested as the easiest way to provide for such modifications, and it is largely true. For example, BIOS calls written for the CGA will work on the EGA and VGA, but not all register functions will. Similarly, plotting a pixel through BIOS uses the same method no matter which adapter/resolution combination is being used, but writing memory varies drastically among the CGA, EGA, and VGA.

BIOS programming also gives greater compatibility between machines and adapters of various manufacturers. Some EGA and VGA registers should be modified only during specific time intervals or must allow recovery time between writes, and BIOS will always take care of these tasks. However, even BIOS programming does not guarantee total compatibility between machines or even easy modification of code for other operating systems.

OS/2 does not use software interrupts (outside the compatibility window) for controlling hardware, and absolutely forbids direct control of the hardware (unless you want to get into the complex world of writing device drivers). Rather, OS/2 relies on calls to the operating system, which resemble calls to external routines in DOS programs: parameters are PUSHed onto the stack and then the appropriate routine is CALLed. Note that Microsoft Windows also uses this technique. If you are writing a program for DOS and are considering adapting it to OS/2, you may want to write macros for each of the operations.

Thus, you could write a macro to set the color and a macro to set a pixel. In early development stages, the macro could call the BIOS interrupt (the set color macro might only put the color number in a variable, and the BIOS routine would do everything else). The next stage might support direct register and memory manipulation, using the color routine to set the appropriate adapter registers, and the plot routine would set registers and write memory. Finally, the OS/2 version would change the macros to PUSH the required parameters and make the subroutine CALL. The line and circle programs in the applications chapter use macros in this manner.

By using macros, you avoid searching through the code for each occurrence of a register or memory access, or INT call. However, you must give appropriate forethought to the structure of your macros — especially deciding which primitive functions to support. For example, if you only look at the BIOS call structure, you might be tempted to combine the color selection and plotting operations. In many cases, it is more efficient (and perhaps even necessary) to separate such functions.

These methods work quite well if you are using a fairly simple, standard set of functions. You can design the macros to work together efficiently and even develop a library of efficient macros for use in other programs. However, if you are pushing the hardware to its limits, the macros may become awkward and slow performance. At this point, you will need to decide whether your application should be adaptable. After all, if you are relying on very specific hardware features, such as vertical retrace detection, it may not be supported on other hardware or operating systems.

BIOS Calls

The EGA BIOS provides 20 basic routines for working with the display. These functions are numbered 0–13h. To access a function, the function number is placed in register AH, and then INT 10h is issued. Most routines require additional values in registers AL, BX, CX, and/or DX. Chapters 2, 3, and 4 give detailed descriptions of each function. You will find notes about each function's operation, along with a table of register contents and programming examples in assembly language and Turbo Pascal. Differences between the old (CGA) and new calls are noted. As mentioned earlier, implementing BIOS calls in macros may help with the transition to register programming or other operating systems.

Each assembly language program is executable so that you will not need to convert the EXE file to a COM file. The Turbo Pascal programs give the same result as the assembly language versions, although the program structure may differ slightly. Note the simplicity of using BIOS calls — the appropriate values are placed in each of the required registers, and an INT 10h is issued. Remember to load each required register with a value; if you have done some CGA BIOS programming it is sometimes easy to miss a required register, especially the page number on graphics modes since the CGA did not support graphics pages.

Text and Graphics Modes

Mode changes are almost always done through BIOS, since it is not usually a time critical operation and is very difficult to program. Two types of modes are available on the IBM graphics cards. The first is an alphanumeric mode (often called "alpha" or "text" mode), which can display only 256 different characters (the EGA can actually display 512 characters with some special programming). The second is graphics mode, which can individually address any picture element ("pel" or "pixel") on the screen, as well as producing 256 predefined characters. Graphics mode is sometimes referred to as APA graphics for "All Points Addressable," because all points (pixels) can be individually addressed (controlled).

The EGA has five alpha modes and seven graphics modes. The alpha modes are numbered 0–3, and 7. Modes 0–3 are identical to modes 0–3 on the CGA, and mode 7 is nearly identical to mode 7 on the monochrome adapter. Likewise, graphics modes 4–6 are identical on the EGA and CGA. The new graphics modes (which provide higher resolution and/or more colors) are numbered 0dh–10h. Once a mode has been selected, information can be written to (or read from) the display through BIOS function calls or direct memory access.

Mode

0	alpha	CGA compatible
1	alpha	CGA compatible
2	alpha	CGA compatible
3	alpha	CGA compatible
4	graphics	CGA compatible
5	graphics	CGA compatible
6	graphics	CGA compatible
7	graphics	monochrome adapter compatible
0dh	graphics	new mode
0eh	graphics	new mode
0fh	graphics	new mode
10h	graphics	new mode

The VGA adds three additional modes — higher resolution monochrome and color graphics modes, as well as a low resolution, 256-color mode. Even though the 256-color mode is low resolution, some pictures will seem more realistic because of the subtle shading that is possible; effective use of shading can increase the apparent resolution of a picture.

IBM will maintain compatibility between BIOS calls and memory addresses for like numbered modes, and you should use these methods whenever possible. By using modes 0–7, and using only the parameters given in the tables throughout this book, your programs will be compatible with existing adapters and should remain compatible with future products.

This chapter covers function calls 0–7, which set the screen environment (mode, cursor location, etc.). These functions are common to all the IBM video adapters, although the VGA and EGA add a few extensions, such as additional display pages.

Function Call 0:   **Set Mode**

Remarks: This function is used to select the operating mode of the card. The basic formats are alphanumeric (no graphics), 320 x 200 graphics, 640 x 200 graphics, and 640 x 350 graphics. The VGA adds 640 x 480 graphics. Characters can be written with functions 9, 0ah, 0eh, and 13h. Points are plotted with function 0ch.

Input: Registers (set before function call):

AH:	set to 0	
AL:	set to the mode number	
	0 and 1 —	40-column alphanumeric (CGA compatible)
	2 and 3 —	80-column alphanumeric (CGA compatible)
	4 and 5 —	320 x 200 4-color graphics limited to 2 palettes (CGA compatible)
	6 —	640 x 200 2-color graphics: one must be black (CGA compatible)
	7 —	monochrome alphanumeric (monochrome adapter compatible)
	8–0ch —	reserved
	0dh —	320 x 200 16 color
	0eh —	640 x 200 16 color

0fh —	640 x 350 monochrome graphics
10h —	640 x 350 color graphics, 4 colors for EGAs with 64K graphics memory, 16 colors if more than 64K is installed.
11h —	640 x 480 monochrome graphics (VGA only)
12h —	640 x 480 16 color (VGA only)
13h —	320 x 200 256 color (VGA only)

Note that only modes 7 and 0fh may be used on an EGA/monochrome monitor combination (and may not be used on an EGA/color monitor combination).

You may set the high bit of AL to 1 if you want to preserve the screen memory (display) while resetting the mode. This is done by adding 80h to the mode number.

The following routines set the mode to 640 x 350 color graphics and draw a line of alternating colors from left to right across row 10 of the screen (using BIOS function call ch). The display will remain in mode 10h when the programs finish. You may return to text mode by using MODE CO80.

Assembly Language Example:

```
data        segment public

            clr     db  16      ;color initially set to 16

data        ends

code        segment public
            assume CS:code

main        proc    far

start:      push    DS
            sub     AX,AX
            push    AX

            mov     AX,data
            mov     DS,AX
            assume  DS:data
```

```
          mov     AH,0        ;select function 0 — set mode
          mov     AL,10h      ;select mode 10h
          int     10h         ;BIOS video call

          mov     CX,639      ;this will be the column

lp:       mov     AH,0ch      ;function call ch — write dot
          mov     AL,clr      ;set color
          dec     AX          ;subtract one from the color
          mov     clr,AL      ;store the new color
          jnz     skip        ;if the color is not 0
                              ; then continue to skip
          mov     clr,16      ;set the color back to 16

skip:     mov     BH,0        ;select page 0
          mov     DX,10       ;set the row to 10
          int     10h         ;BIOS video call
          loop    lp          ;decrement CX (next column)

          ret

main
          endp

code      ends

end       start
```

Turbo Pascal Example:

```
          type
                  regs = record
                                  AX,BX,CX,DX,BP,SI,DI,DS,ES,
                                  FLAGS: INTEGER;
                  end;

          var
                  reg: regs;
                  column,color: integer;

          begin
                  reg.AX := $0010;
                  intr($10,reg);

          color :=  16;
          for column:= 639 downto 0 do
```

```
                    begin
                    color := color - 1;
                    reg.AX := $0c00 + color;
                    if color = 0 then
                    color := 16;
                    reg.BX := 0;
                    reg.DX := 10;
                    reg.CX := column;
                    intr($10,reg);
                    end;
            end.
```

Function Call 1:   **Set Cursor Type**

Remarks: This function sets the size of the cursor. You may
specify a starting line and an ending line, which fills a
rectangular area of the character box (note that the cursor need not start at the top or end at bottom — it is possible for the cursor to be in the middle of the box). Note
that there is no cursor in graphics modes.

The starting and ending lines require only the low
four bits. Bits 5 and 6 should always be set to 0. Line 0
is the top line of the box. The cursor can be turned off by
setting the beginning and ending lines below the character box. On the EGA, setting the starting line to a higher
value than the ending line will cause the cursor to wrap
from the bottom of the box to the top, giving a double
line (you could also think of it as a reverse video cursor
with the black starting at the ending line and ending at
the starting line). The VGA does not support a double
cursor; it will disappear if the starting line is larger than
the ending line.

The cursor may exhibit unusual behavior on the
ECD. Because compatibility with the old color alpha
modes requires an eight-line cursor, only eight lines are
available for setting. On the ECD, alpha modes use a 14 -
line character box — lines 0–4 reference the top five
lines and lines 5–7 reference the bottom three lines. Any
range which contains both lines 4 and 5 will also fill the
six lines between them (try setting the cursor to lines 4
and 5, and observe the large cursor block this creates).

Input: Registers (set before function call):

        AH: set to 1
        CH: starting line number
        CL: ending line number

The following routines create a cursor consisting of the top two lines of the character box:

Assembly Language Example:

```
code        segment public
            assume CS:code

main        proc    far

start:      push    DS
            sub     AX,AX
            push    AX

            mov     AH,1        ;function 1 — set cursor mode
            mov     CX,1        ;start line 0, stop line 1 (CL=1)
            int     10h         ;BIOS video call

            ret

main        endp

code        ends

end         start
```

Turbo Pascal Example:

```
            type
                    regs = record
                            AX,BX,CX,DX,BP,SI,DI,DS,
                            ES,FLAGS: INTEGER;
                    end;

            var
                    reg: regs;

            begin
                    reg.AX := $0100;
                    reg.CX := $0001;
```

```
                    intr($10,reg);
          end.
```

Function Call 2:   **Set Cursor Position**

Remarks: Give the coordinates for the cursor's position on
             the screen. Row 0 is the top of the screen, and column 0
             is the left side of the screen.

Input: Registers (set before function call):

             AH: set to 2
             DH: row number
             DL: column number
             BH: page number (see function 5 for a descrip-
                     tion of pages)

The following routines set the cursor to row 5, column 10 of page 0:

Assembly Language Example:

```
code        segment public
            assume CS:code

main        proc    far

start:      push    DS
            sub     AX,AX
            push    AX

            mov     AH,2        ;function 2 — set cursor position
            mov     DH,05       ;row 5
            mov     DL,0ah      ;column 10
            mov     BH,0        ;page 0
            int     10h         ;BIOS video call

            ret

main        endp

code        ends

end         start
```

Turbo Pascal Example:

```
type        regs = record
                        AX,BX,CX,DX,BP,SI,DI,DS,
                        ES,FLAGS: INTEGER;

end;

var
            reg: regs;

begin
            reg.AX := $0200;
            reg.DX := $050a;
            reg.BX := $0000;
            intr($10,reg);

end.
```

Function Call 3:   Read Cursor Position

Remarks: This function reports the current location of the
            cursor on the screen. It also reports the current cursor
            type (see function 1 above).

Input: Registers (set before function call):

            AH: set to 3
            BH: page number (see function 5 for a
                    description of pages)

Output: Registers (read after function call):

            DH: Current row
            DL: Current column
            CH: Starting line
            CL: Ending line

The following routines set the cursor to row 5, column 10, get the
cursor location on page 0, and then print a message (giving the new
coordinates) at the current position:

```
data        segment public

            msg     db          'The cursor is at row    '
                    db          'and column    '
```

```
data        ends

code        segment public
            assume CS:code

main        proc    far

start:      push    DS
            sub     AX,AX
            push    AX

            mov     AX,data
            mov     DS,AX
            assume  DS:data

            mov     AH,2        ;function 2 — set cursor
            mov     DH,05       ;row 5
            mov     DL,0ah      ;column 10
            mov     BH,0        ;page 0
            int     10h         ;BIOS video call

            mov     AH,3        ;function 3 — read cursor
                                    position
            mov     BH,0        ;page 0
            int     10h         ;BIOS video call
                                ;DH now contains the row
                                ;DL now contains the column

            mov     AL,DL       ;mov column into AL
            mov     BX,offset msg[35]      ;offset of ASCII #
            call    bin2asc     ;conv. binary to ASCII
            mov     AL,DH       ;move row into AL
            sub     BX,14       ;offset for ASCII #
            call    bin2asc     ;convert again

            mov     AX,data     ;get data segment location
            mov     ES,AX       ;set ES for next function call
            assume  ES:data
            mov     AH,13h      ;function 13h — write string
            mov     AL,0        ;cursor does not move
                                ;string of characters only
                                ;attribute in BL
            mov     BH,0        ;page 0
            mov     BL,0fh      ;high intensity white
            mov     BP,offset msg      ;ES:BP points to string
            mov     CX,37       ;length of string
```

```
                int     10h             ;BIOS video call
                ret

main            endp

bin2asc         proc    near

COMMENT*                This binary to ASCII conversion routine is
                written for this program and is limited to
                numbers less than 100.
                AL: 8 bit value to convert
                BX: offset in DS which receives a 2 byte ASCII
                value
                *
                mov     AH,0
                mov     DL,10
                div     DL              ;convert to decimal digits
                add     AX,3030h    ;add 30h to get ASCII codes
                mov     [BX],AL     ;write 10's place
                mov     [BX+1],AH ;write 1's place
                ret

bin2asc         endp

code            ends

end             start
```

Turbo Pascal Example:

```
type
                regs = record
                        AX,BX,CX,DX,BP,SI,DI,DS,ES,
                        FLAGS: INTEGER;
                end;

                var
                        reg: regs;
                        row, col: integer;

                begin
                        reg.AX := $0200    {set cursor};
                        reg.DX := $050a;
```

```
reg.BX := $0000;
intr($10,reg);

reg.AX := $0300     (get cursor);
reg.BX := $0000;
intr($10,reg);
row := reg.DX div $100;
col := reg.DX mod $100;



Write ('The cursor is at row ',row);
Write (' and column ',col);

end.
```

Function Call 4:   **Read Light Pen Position**

Remarks: This function reports whether the light pen has
been triggered (the pen's switch has been pushed) and
the row and column where the triggering occurred. Note
that in the registers, CH is used for reporting the row of
the compatibility modes (4–6) and CX is used for the
new modes.

Notes: The VGA does not support a light pen.

Input: Registers (set before function call):

AH: set to 4

Output: Registers (read after function call):

AH: 0 means the light pen has not been trig-
gered (invalid values in registers), and 1
means the pen has been triggered (the
following registers contain valid data).
DH: character row
DL: character column
CH: pixel row (compatibility modes)
CX: pixel row (new graphics modes)
BX: pixel column

Function Call 5:   Select Active Display Page

Remarks: The adapter may have several pages (or screens)
of information in memory. Only one page is visible at
any one time — this is called the active display. Most of
the functions which allow you to modify the screen
(write characters, plot points, move the cursor, etc.) also
let you choose which page to modify and thus an in-
visible screen may be changed. Through this feature,
you may display one page while another is being
created, and then immediately switch to the new screen
(a technique useful for animation or "slide shows"). This
function lets you choose which screen is displayed.
Usually, screen 0 is the only screen displayed and
modified.

The CGA is limited to four pages in modes 2 and 3, and
the monochrome adapter supports only one page.

Note that in the table below, the range of page numbers
which can be used in AL is shown. A "0" means one page
(number 0) is available.

Input: Registers (set before function call):

AH: set to 5
AL: page number to display

modes   page numbers available

modes	64K	128K	256K	
0–1	0–7	0–7	0–7	
2–3	0–3	0–7	0–7	
4–6	0	0	0	
7	0–3	0–7	0–7	
0dh	0–1	0–3	0–7	
0eh	0	0–1	0–3	
0fh	0	0–1	0–1	
10h	0	0	0–1	
11h			0	(VGA only)
12h			0	(VGA only)
13h			0	(VGA only)

Assembly Language Example:

This program flips through four video pages,
pausing on each page. The pause becomes shorter with
each successive loop. One word appears on each page,
forming the message "This shows four pages."

```
data        segment public

            msg1    db          ' This'
            msg2    db          ' shows'
            msg3    db          ' four '
            msg4    db          'pages.'
            pse     dw          0F000h
                                ;length of display pause


data        ends

code        segment public
            assume CS:code

main        proc    far

start:      push    DS
            sub     AX,AX
            push    AX

            mov     AX,data     ;get data segment location
            mov     ES,AX       ;set ES for next function call
            assume  ES:data

            mov     AX,data
            mov     DS,AX
            assume  DS:data

            mov     AX,3        ;mode 3 (alphanumeric)
            int     10h

            mov     DH,08       ;row 8
            mov     DL,0ah      ;column 10
            mov     BH,3        ;page 3
            mov     BP,offset msg1      ;ES:BP points to string
            mov     BL,0fh      ;high intensity white
            mov     CX,6        ;length of string

;load the four pages with the message
```

```
loop:       mov     AL,1            ;cursor moves
                                    ;string of characters only
                                    ;attribute in BL
            mov     AH,13h          ;function 13h — write string
            int     10h             ;BIOS video call
            add     BP,6            ;point to next message
            add     DL,6            ;move the cursor for next page
            dec     BH              ;point to the next page
            cmp     BP,offset msg4
            jbe     loop

;display the four pages

dsp:        mov     CX,4

lp2:        mov     AL,CL
            dec     AX
            mov     AH,5
            int     10h
            push    CX
            mov     CX,2            ;pause multiplier
                                    ; (for longer time)

ps1:        push    CX
            mov     CX,pse          ;pause length

ps2:        loop    ps2             ;empty loop for pause
            pop     CX
            loop    ps1             ;loop through the multiplier
            pop     CX
            loop    lp2
            mov     AX,pse
            sub     AX,1000h
            mov     pse,ax
            cmp     AX,0
            ja      dsp

;reset to page 0 before returning to DOS

            mov     AL,0
            mov     AH,5
            int     10h

            ret

main        endp
```

code	ends
end	start

Function Call 6:   Scroll Active Page Up

Remarks: This function scrolls the text on the screen – lines move from the bottom of the screen toward the top, and blank lines are inserted at the bottom. Note that corners of a window can be specified, so that only a portion of the screen scrolls. Register AL is set to the number of lines to scroll; using 0 will clear the entire window.

Input: Registers (set before function call):

AH:	set to 6
AL:	number of lines to scroll (0 clears the window)
BH:	character attribute for new lines (see function 8 below)
CH:	top row of the window
CL:	left column of the window
DH:	bottom row of the window
DL:	right column of the window

Assembly Language Example:

This program prints the message "This line will scroll (except for this part)" and scrolls the first part up one line. A second line is printed which does not scroll, and you can see the effect of a scroll window.

```
data        segment public

            msg1    db      'This line will scroll (except for '
                    db      'this part)'
            msg2    db      'This line will not scroll'

data        ends

code        segment public
            assume CS:code

main        proc    far
```

```
start:      push    DS
            sub     AX,AX
            push    AX

            mov     AX,data         ;get data segment location
            mov     ES,AX           ;set ES for next function call
            assume  ES:data

            mov     AX,data
            mov     DS,AX
            assume  DS:data

            mov     AX,3            ;mode 3 (alphanumeric)
            int     10h

            mov     DH,12           ;row 12
            mov     DL,10           ;column 10
            mov     BH,0            ;page 0
            mov     BP,offset msg1      ;ES:BP points to string
            mov     BL,0fh          ;high intensity white
            mov     CX,44           ;length of string
            mov     AL,1            ;cursor moves
                                    ;string of characters only
                                    ;attribute in BL
            mov     AH,13h          ;function 13h — write string
            int     10h             ;BIOS video call

            mov     DH,13           ;row 13
            mov     DL,10           ;column 10
            mov     BH,0            ;page 0
            mov     BP,offset msg2      ;ES:BP points to string
            mov     BL,0fh          ;high intensity white
            mov     CX,25           ;length of string
            mov     AL,1            ;cursor moves
                                    ;string of characters only
                                    ;attribute in BL
            mov     AH,13h          ;function 13h — write string
            int     10h             ;BIOS video call

            mov     CX,2            ;pause multiplier
                                    ; (for longer time)

ps1:        push    CX
            mov     CX,0ffffh       ;pause length
```

```
ps2:        loop    ps2         ;empty loop for pause
            pop     CX
            loop    ps1         ;loop through the multiplier

            mov     CX,0        ;upper left corner at 0,0
            mov     DH,12       ;right corner at row 12
            mov     DL,31       ;column 31
            mov     AL,1        ;move 1 line
            mov     BH,0fh      ;attribute for new line
            mov     AH,6        ;scroll up
            int     10h

            ret

main        endp

code        ends

end         start
```

Function Call 7:   Scroll Active Page Down

Remarks: This function scrolls the text on the screen — lines
            move from the top of the screen toward the bottom, and
            blank lines are inserted at the top. It works in the same
            manner as function 6.

Input: Registers (set before function call):

            AH: set to 7
            AL: number of lines to scroll (0 clears the
                    window)
            BH: character attribute for new lines
                    (see function 8 below)
            CH: top row of the window
            CL: left column of the window
            DH: bottom row of the window
            DL: right column of the window

Assembly Language Example:

            This program prints the message "This line will
            scroll (except for this part)" and scrolls the first part
```
```

down one line. A second line is printed which does not scroll, and you can see the effect of a scroll window.

```
data      segment public

          msg1    db        'This line will not scroll '

          msg2    db        'This line will scroll (except for '
                  db        'this part)'

data      ends

code      segment public
          assume CS:code

main      proc    far

start:    push    DS
          sub     AX,AX
          push    AX

          mov     AX,data       ;get data segment location
          mov     ES,AX         ;set ES for next function call
          assume  ES:data

          mov     AX,data
          mov     DS,AX
          assume  DS:data

          mov     AX,3          ;mode 3 (alphanumeric)
          int     10h

          mov     DH,12         ;row 12
          mov     DL,10         ;column 10
          mov     BH,0          ;page 0
          mov     BP,offset msg1    ;ES:BP points to string
          mov     BL,0fh        ;high intensity white
          mov     CX,25         ;length of string
          mov     AL,1          ;cursor moves
                                ;string of characters only
                                ;attribute in BL
          mov     AH,13h        ;function 13h — write string
          int     10h           ;BIOS video call

          mov     DH,13         ;row 13
          mov     DL,10         ;column 10
```

```
          mov     BH,0          ;page 0
          mov     BP,offset msg2      ;ES:BP points to string
          mov     BL,0fh        ;high intensity white
          mov     CX,44         ;length of string
          mov     AL,1          ;cursor moves
                                ;string of characters only
                                ;attribute in BL
          mov     AH,13h        ;function 13h — write string
          int     10h           ;BIOS video call

          mov     CX,2          ;pause multiplier
                                ; (for longer time)

ps1:      push    CX
          mov     CX,0ffffh     ;pause length

ps2:      loop    ps2           ;empty loop for pause
          pop     CX
          loop    ps1           ;loop through the multiplier

          mov     CH,13         ;upper left corner row 13
          mov     CL,0          ;column 0
          mov     DH,24         ;lower right corner at row 24
          mov     DL,31         ;column 31
          mov     AL,1          ;move 1 line
          mov     BH,0fh        ;attribute for new line
          mov     AH,7          ;scroll down
          int     10h

                                ;move cursor so DOS doesn't
                                overwrite last line

          mov     AH,2          ;function 2 — set cursor
          mov     DH,15         ;row 15
          mov     DL,1          ;column 1
          mov     BH,0          ;page 0
          int     10h           ;BIOS video call

          ret

main      endp

code      ends

end       start
```

Of the display management functions (0–7), the most important is the Set Mode function. Programs usually do not require a particularly fast reset, and using the BIOS call guarantees the mode will be properly set on all adapters that support the requested mode. Functions 1–7 are more useful in prototyping — if you write programs that directly manipulate display memory, they are of little use.

3

BIOS Screen I/O

The next set of BIOS function calls (numbers 8-fh) works directly with the display image, either by writing or reading screen contents or color scheme. The exception is function call fh, which returns the current video mode. As with function calls 0–7, the video I/O functions are supported by all of the IBM adapters. The video I/O routines are notoriously slow, and most programmers bypass these routines once the general prototyping is finished. However, some of the routines can be very useful even in finished applications.

For example, the character writing routines work in all modes. This can be especially helpful if you need to display text in graphics modes, and you do not require a great deal of sophistication (such as different sizes or pixel alignment). Graphics mode character I/O routines are not easy to write, and may not be worth the effort required.

Function Call 8:   **Read Attribute/Character at Current Cursor Position**

Remarks: You can use this function to read a character on any of the pages. The information returned applies to the character at the cursor position of the page selected (see function 2 for setting the cursor position).

             The attribute is a one byte value which describes the character and background according to the following diagram:

```
  7        6 5 4     3      2 1 0
┌──────────┬──────────┬──────┬──────────┐
│  blink   │background│inten-│foreground│
│          │  color   │ sity │  color   │
└──────────┴──────────┴──────┴──────────┘
```

For color monitors, the three color bits for background and foreground give eight colors. For monochrome monitors, the three background bits should be either all 0 (black) or all 1 (colored), and the three foreground bits should be either 000 for black foreground, 001 for underline, or 111 for a normal (colored) foreground. The attribute byte is only meaningful in alpha modes. See function calls 10h and 11h for additional notes about attributes and character codes.

Input: Registers (set before function call):

AH: set to 8
BH: page number (see function 5 for a description of pages)

Output: Registers (read after function call):

AL: ASCII code of the character
AH: In alpha mode, this will contain the attribute of the character.

Assembly Language Example:

This program reports the ASCII character and attribute byte value at Row 5 and Column 15. You might want to try this program after running one of the following two examples (function call 9 or 0ah). If you try both examples (functions 9 and 0ah) use this order: functions 0ah, 8, 9, and 8. This will demonstrate the changing attribute byte.

```
data      segment public

          msg    db    'Row 5, Column 15 contains ASCII '
                 db    'character '
          char   db    3 dup (?)
                 db    ', and attribute value '
          attr   db    3 dup (?)
```

```
            m_len     equ
                      $-msg          ;creates a constant from
                                     ;here to message start
                                     ;(message length)

data        ends

code        segment public
            assume CS:code

main        proc      far

start:      push      DS
            sub       AX,AX
            push      AX

            mov       AX,data
            mov       DS,AX
            assume    DS:data

            mov       AX,data
            mov       ES,AX
            assume    ES:data

            mov       BH,0           ;page 0
            mov       DH,5           ;row 5
            mov       DL,15          ;column 15
            mov       AH,2           ;set cursor position
            int       10h            ;BIOS video call

            mov       BH,0           ;page 0
            mov       AH,8           ;function call 8 — read
                                     ;character and attribute
            int       10h            ;BIOS video call
            mov       BL,AH          ;save attr in BL, temporarily

            mov       DI,offset char
            call      bin2asc
            mov       AL,BL          ;get attribute
            mov       DI,offset attr
            call      bin2asc

            mov       DH,20          ;row 20
            mov       DL,0           ;column 0
            mov       BH,0           ;page 0
            mov       BP,offset msg     ;ES:BP points to string
            mov       BL,0fh         ;high intensity white
```

```
        mov     CX,m_len    ;length of string
        mov     AL,1        ;cursor moves
                            ;string of characters only
                            ;attribute in BL
        mov     AH,13h      ;function 13h — write string
        int     10h         ;BIOS video call

        ret

main    endp

bin2asc proc    near
```

COMMENT*   This binary to ASCII conversion routine is
           written for this program and is limited to
           numbers less than 256.
           AL: 8-bit value to convert
           DI: offset in DS which receives a 2-byte ASCII
           value
           *

```
        xor     AH,AH       ;0 in AH
        mov     DL,100
        div     DL          ;convert to decimal 100's
        add     AL,30h      ;convert 100's place to ASCII
        mov     [DI],AL     ;write 100's place
        mov     AL,AH
        xor     AH,AH       ;0 in AH
        mov     DL,10
        div     DL          ;convert to decimal digits
        add     AX,3030h    ;add 30h to get ASCII codes
        mov     [DI+1],AL   ;write 10's place
        mov     [DI+2],AH   ;write 1's place
        ret

        mov     DH,21       ;row 21
        mov     DL,0        ;column 0
        mov     AH,2        ;function call 2 — set cursor
        int     10h         ;BIOS video call

bin2asc endp

code    ends

end     start
```

Function Call 9:   **Write Attribute/Character at Current Cursor Position**

Remarks: You can use this function to write a character (or several copies of a character) to any of the pages. The character(s) will appear at the current cursor position, which can be set through function call 2.

The attribute is a one byte value which describes the character and background according to the following diagram for the alpha modes:

7	6 5 4	3	2 1 0
blink	background color	inten-sity	foreground color

For color monitors, the three color bits for background and foreground give eight colors. For monochrome monitors, the three background bits should be either all 0 (black) or all 1 (colored), and the three foreground bits should be either 000 for black foreground, 001 for underline, or 111 for a normal (colored) foreground.

In graphics modes, the attribute byte is used to set the color of the character. Setting bit 7 of the attribute byte will cause an exclusive or at the cursor location, thus preventing lines within the character box from being erased. See function calls 10h and 11h for additional notes about attributes and character codes.

In alpha modes, writing more copies of a character than will fit on the current line will cause a wraparound to the next line. In graphics modes, all of the copies must fit on the current line.

Note: The cursor position remains unchanged after the call is completed (even when multiple copies of a character are made). Character positioning must be done by the program.

Control codes are printed as display characters, so backspaces, carriage returns, linefeeds, etc. must be done through cursor positioning.

Input: Registers (set before function call):

AH: set to 9
AL: ASCII code of the character
BH: page number (see function 5 for a
       description of pages)
       Mode 13h uses BH for the background
       color.
BL: attribute of character
CX: number of characters to write

Assembly Language Example:

This program prints a message, character by character, changing the attribute (color) on each character. Note the effect of the control codes 7, 10, and 13. Compare the results to functions ah, eh, and 13h.

```
data        segment public

msg         db      'This line demonstrates printing '
            db      'ASCII 7 (',7,'), 10 (',10,'), and'
            db      ' 13 (',13,').'

m_len       equ     $-msg       ;creates a constant from
                                ;here to message start
                                ;(message length)

data        ends

code        segment public
            assume CS:code

main        proc    far

start:      push    DS
            sub     AX,AX
            push    AX
```

```
                mov     AX,data
                mov     DS,AX
                assume  DS:data

                mov     DH,05        ;row 5 (for call 2)
                mov     DL,0         ;column 0 (for call 2)
                mov     CX,m_len     ;number of iterations
                mov     BP,offset msg        ;pointer to message
                mov     BL,1         ;initialize BL to 1
                                     ; start with color 1

lp1:            inc     DX           ;next column
                mov     AH,2         ;function 2 — set cursor
                int     10h          ;BIOS video call

                push    CX           ;save iteration count
                mov     CX,1         ;write one character
                mov     BH,0         ;page 0
                mov     AL,msg[BP]          ;get ASCII code
                mov     AH,9         ;function call 9
                int     10h          ;BIOS video call
                inc     BP           ;point to next character
                inc     BX           ;next color (add 1 to #)
                cmp     BL,15        ;if 15
                jbe     skp          ; skip next section
                mov     BL,1         ;if 15, color set to 1

skp:            pop     CX           ;restore iteration count
                loop    lp1

                mov     DH,21        ;row 21
                mov     DL,0         ;column 0
                mov     AH,2         ;function call 2 — set cursor
                int     10h          ;BIOS video call

                ret

main            endp

code            ends

end             start
```

Function Call ah: **Write Character Only at Current Cursor Position**

Remarks: This function call is identical to function call 9 above, except that the attribute cannot be set (existing attributes remain unchanged).

Input: Registers (set before function call):
AH: set to ah
AL: ASCII code of the character
BH: page number (see function 5 for a description of pages)
CX: number of characters to write

Assembly Language Example:

Note: This program is the same as the one for function call 9, except that the function call number has changed. The output picks up the attributes currently in effect. Thus, if you do a CLS command before using this program, the output will be in the normal white color. If you run the program from the previous example first, the display will remain unchanged, since the new characters will pick up the old (multicolored) attributes.

```
data       segment public

msg        db      'This line demonstrates
                      printing'
           db      'ASCII 7 (',7,'), 10 (',10,'), and'
           db      ' 13 (',13,').'

m_len      equ     $-msg          ;creates a constant from
                                  ;here to message start
                                  ;(message length)

data       ends

code       segment public
           assume CS:code

main       proc    far

start:     push    DS
           sub     AX,AX
           push    AX
```

```
            mov     AX,data
            mov     DS,AX
            assume  DS:data

            mov     DH,05      ;row 5 (for call 2)
            mov     DL,0       ;column 0 (for call 2)
            mov     CX,m_len   ;number of iterations
            mov     BP,offset msg      ;pointer to message
            mov     BL,1       ;initialize BL to 1
                               ; start with color 1

lp1:        inc     DX         ;next column
            mov     AH,2       ;function 2 — set cursor
            int     10h        ;BIOS video call

            push    CX         ;save iteration count
            mov     CX,1       ;write one character
            mov     BH,0       ;page 0
            mov     AL,msg[BP]        ;get ASCII code
            mov     AH,0ah     ;function call 0ah
                               ;note that the attribute
                               ;byte (BL) has no effect
            int     10h        ;BIOS video call
            inc     BP         ;point to next character
            inc     BX         ;next color (add 1 to #)
            cmp     BL,15      ;if 15
            jbe     skp        ; skip next section
            mov     BL,1       ;if 15, color set to 1

skp:        pop     CX         ;restore iteration count
            loop    lp1

            mov     DH,21      ;row 21
            mov     DL,0       ;column 0
            mov     AH,2       ;function call 2 — set cursor
            int     10h        ;BIOS video call

            ret

main        endp

code        ends

end         start
```

Function Call bh: Set Color Palette

Remarks: This function call applies only to compatibility
                modes; see function call 10h to set the palette for the
                new modes.

                Register BH is set to access either the background
                color (0) or the set of colors to be used for 320 x 200
                graphics (1). Any value from 0 to 127 is legal, although 0
                and 1 are sufficient (even numbers work as 0 and odd
                numbers work as 1).

Input: Registers (set before function call):

                AH: set to bh
                BH: palette color ID
                BL: for BH = 0, the background color (0-15) in
                        graphics mode, or the border color (0-31)
                        in alpha mode. Note that background
                        color is a character attribute in alpha
                        modes (see function call 8).

                        for BH = 1, 0 selects green, red, and brown;
                        and 1 selects cyan, magenta, and white.
                        These colors are numbers 1, 2, and 3,
                        respectively — color 0 is the background
                        color.

Assembly Language Example:

                This program prints a line of colored dots across
                the screen in CGA emulation mode, and then changes
                the palette from the default (cyan, magenta, white) to
                green, red, and brown.

```
data        segment public

            clr     db          3           ;color initially set to 3

data        ends

code        segment public
            assume CS:code

main        proc    far
```

```
start:      push    DS
            sub     AX,AX
            push    AX

            mov     AX,data
            mov     DS,AX
            assume  DS:data

            mov     AH,0        ;select function 0 — set mode
            mov     AL,5        ;select mode 5
            int     10h         ;BIOS video call

            mov     BH,1        ;select graphics color palette
            mov     BL,1        ;select cyan, magenta, blue
            mov     AH,0bh      ;set palette
            int     10h         ;BIOS video call

            mov     BH,0        ;select background color
            mov     BL,0        ;black
            mov     AH,0bh      ;set palette
            int     10h         ;BIOS video call

            mov     CX,319      ;this will be the column

lp:         mov     AH,0ch      ;function call ch — write dot
            mov     AL,clr      ;set color
            dec     AX          ;subtract one from the color
            mov     clr,AL      ;store the new color
            jnz     skip        ;if the color is not 0
                                ; then continue to skip
            mov     clr,3       ;set the color back to 3

skip:       mov     BH,0        ;select page 0
            mov     DX,10       ;set the row to 10
            int     10h         ;BIOS video call
            loop    lp          ;decrement CX (next column)

            mov     CX,4        ;pause multiplier
                                ; (for longer time)

ps1:        push    CX
            mov     CX,0ffffh   ;pause length

ps2:        loop    ps2         ;empty loop for pause
            pop     CX
            loop    ps1         ;loop through the multiplier
```

```
        mov     BH,1        ;select graphics color palette
        mov     BL,0        ;select green, red, and brown
        mov     AH,0bh      ;set palette
        int     10h         ;BIOS video call

        mov     DH,10       ;row 10
        mov     DL,0        ;column 0
        mov     BH,0        ;page 0
        mov     AH,2        ;function call 2 — set cursor
        int     10h         ;BIOS video call

        ret

main    endp

code    ends

end     start
```

Function Call ch: **Write Dot**

Remarks: This function call is used to plot a point to any page
            in graphics modes. Column 0 is the left side of the
            screen and row 0 is the top of the screen (note that this
            differs from most coordinate systems, which use row 0
            as the bottom).

            Setting bit 7 of the color number (register AL) will
            cause the dot to be exclusive OR'ed with the current
            value.

Note: Register BH (page number) is not supported on the
            CGA, since it does not have graphics pages. However, it
            must be set on the EGA and VGA.

Input: Registers (set before function call):

            AH: set to ch
            AL: color number
            BH: page number (see function 5 for a descrip-
                    tion of pages)
            CX: pixel column number (0–319 or 0–639)
            DX: pixel row number (0–199, 0–349, or 0–479)

            The Assembly Language Example for function
            call 0 (set mode), uses the write dot call. Appendix A

contains a similar program which writes the pixels directly to memory. The example for function call dh (read dot), also uses the write dot call. However, you will be executing the read dot program, so you should first run the set mode program.

Function Call dh: Read Dot

Remarks: This function call is used to get the color of a point of any page in graphics modes. Column 0 is the left side of the screen and row 0 is the top of the screen (note that this differs from most coordinate systems, which use row 0 as the bottom).

Note: Register BH (page number) is not supported on the CGA, since it does not have graphics pages. However, it must be set on the EGA and VGA.

Input: Registers (set before function call):

AH: set to dh
BH: page number (see function 5 for a description of pages)
CX: pixel column number (0–319 or 0–639)
DX: pixel row number (0–199, 0–349, or 0–479)

Output: Registers (read after function call):

AL: color value of the dot

Assembly Language Example:

This program copies row 10 to row 20. The display must be in high-resolution graphics mode; it is intended for use after running the set mode (function 0) example.

```
data        segment public

    clr     db      16      ;color initially 16

    msg     db      'The mode must be set to high '
            db      'resolution.'
            m_end   label   byte

data        ends
```

```
code            segment public
                assume CS:code

main            proc    far

start:          push    DS
                sub     AX,AX
                push    AX

                mov     AX,data
                mov     DS,AX
                assume  DS:data
                mov     AH,0fh      ;function 0fh current mode
                int     10h         ;BIOS video call
                cmp     AL,0eh      ;is the mode less than 0eh?
                jl      bad_mode
                cmp     AL,13h      ;is the mode low res, 256 color?
                je      bad_mode

                mov     CX,639      ;this will be the column

lp:             mov     AH,0dh      ;function call dh read dot
                mov     BH,0        ;select page 0
                mov     DX,10       ;set the row to 10
                int     10h         ;BIOS video call
                                    ;color now in AL
                mov     AH,0ch      ;function call ch — write dot
                mov     DX,20       ;set the row to 20
                int     10h         ;BIOS video call
                loop    lp          ;decrement CX (next column)

                ret
bad_mode:

                mov     AX,data
                mov     ES,AX
                assume  ES:data
                mov     AH,3        ;function 02h — read cursor pos.
                mov     BH,0        ;page 0
                int     10h         ;BIOS video call
                                    ;DX contains cursor position
                mov     DL,0        ;set to column 0
                mov     AX,1300h    ;write string (all
                                    ;char. data)
                mov     BH,0        ;page 0
                mov     BL,3        ;color 3
                mov     BP,offset msg           ;ES:BP points to text
```

```
          mov     CX,offset m_end-msg        ;length of the text
                                             ;DX already set

          int     10h         ;BIOS video call

          ret

main      endp

code      ends

end       start
```

Function Call eh: **Write Teletype to Active Page**

Remarks: This function is used as a teletype emulation: A
             character is written and the cursor is moved to the next
             position. Unlike the other write character functions, this
             function interprets the bell, carriage return, and
             linefeed characters as commands rather than characters
             from the IBM set.

Note: This function will write only to the active
             display page.

Input: Registers (set before function call):

             AH: set to eh
             AL: ASCII code of the character
             BL: foreground color (works in graphics
                    mode only)

Assembly Language Example:

             This program prints a full string (message) at once.
             Note the effect of the control codes 7, 10, and 13. Com-
             pare the results to functions 9, ah, and 13h.

data   segment public

```
          msg     db          'This line demonstrates printing '
                  db          'ASCII 7 (',7,'), 10 (',10,'), and '
                  db          ' 13 (',13,').'

          m_len   equ $-msg   ;creates a constant from
                              ;here to message start
                              ;(message length)
```

```
data        ends

code        segment public
            assume CS:code

main        proc    far

start:      push    DS
            sub     AX,AX
            push    AX
            mov     AX,data
            mov     DS,AX
            assume  DS:data
            mov     DH,05       ;row 5 (for call 2)
            mov     DL,0        ;column 0 (for call 2)
            mov     CX,m_len    ;number of iterations
            mov     BP,offset msg       ;pointer to message

            mov     BL,1        ;initialize BL to 1
                                ; start with color 1
            inc     DX          ;next column
            mov     AH,2        ;function 2 set cursor
            int     10h         ;BIOS video call

;NOTE the cursor is set outside the loop —
; compare this to the write character/attribute
; (function 9) program.

lp1:        mov     BH,0        ;page 0
            mov     AL,msg[BP]          ;get ASCII code
            mov     AH,0eh      ;function call 0eh
            int     10h         ;BIOS video call
            inc     BP          ;point to next character
            inc     BX          ;next color (add 1 to #)
            cmp     BL,15       ;if 15
            jbe     skp         ; skip next section
            mov     BL,1        ;if 15, color set to 1

;NOTE the color does not work in alpha modes.
; Try it, then use the set mode (function 0)
; program to set graphics mode and you will see
; the colors appear.

skp:        loop    lp1
            mov     DH,21       ;row 21
            mov     DL,0        ;column 0
            mov     AH,2        ;function call 2 set cursor
```

```
int      10h        ;BIOS video call

ret
main     endp
code     ends
end      start
```

Function Call fh: **Current Video State**

Remarks: This function returns information about the current
             mode setting.

Input: Registers (set before function call):

             AH: set to fh

Output: Registers (read after function call):

             AL: current mode number (see function
                    call 0 for a description of modes)
             AH: number of character columns displayed
             BH: number of the active page (see function
                    call 5 for a description of pages).

The Assembly Language Example for function call dh (read dot)
uses the current video state function call.

This completes the base set of BIOS function calls. The differences
between the EGA/VGA and monochrome/CGA calls have been mini-
mal, limited to extended ranges, either in the number of pages or
pixels available. All of the remaining functions are unique to the
newer adapters (the PC Jr and Model 30 also support some of the new
calls, but we will not be discussing these models).

4

BIOS EGA/VGA Extensions

We have now arrived at the new functions supported by the EGA and VGA. These calls support a very diverse group of operations, from palette and character modification to returning adapter configuration data. You will probably use the status routines most frequently — especially if your application will automatically configure its display environment.

Additionally, you may make frequent use of the Set Palette function. Changing the palette is not usually a time sensitive operation, and when execution time is not critical, it is best to let BIOS perform the task to enhance compatibility and reduce development time.

Function Call 10h: Set Palette Registers

Remarks: This function call is used to change any one (or all) of the colors to another color and to set the border color.

Notes: In 16-color modes, the palette register number is the same as the color number. In compatibility modes, registers 1–3 form the colors of palette 1, and colors 4–6 form the colors of palette 0. If the ECD is used in graphics mode 10h with 64K on the EGA, the following scheme is used:

Palette register	Color numbers:
0	0,2,8,10
1	1,3,9,11
4	4,6,12,14
7	5,7,13,15

The palette registers will return to the default values whenever the mode is reset. When using this function to change the palette, it should be used after every reset. Alternately, you may change the defaults by making a new parameter table and changing the BIOS SAVE_PTR table (a detailed explanation of this method appears in Chapter 12). The VGA can disable the default palettes through Alternate Select (function call 12h, BL=31h)

In addition to the standard palette registers, the VGA has a Digital to Analog Converter which also controls the displayed color. The DAC uses six bits for the intensity of each color (red, green, and blue), resulting in an 18-bit color value (262,144 colors). The DAC has 256 registers, and each register may hold a different color value. Thus mode 13h may use 256 colors out of a possible 262,144.

In 16-color VGA modes, the Palette register selects 16-registers of a 64-register DAC subset (and the ability to switch between four subsets). Alternately, the palette register may select 16 registers from a 16 register subset (with 16 subsets available). The default after a mode set (except for mode 13h) is 16/64/4; only subset 0 is initialized and used.

Input: Registers (set before function call):

AH: set to 10h

Function 0
Set individual
palette
register: Registers (set before function call):

Note: Although this function is primarily intended for changing the palette registers, it can be used to change any of the attribute registers (see Chapter 4 for a description of each attribute register).

AL: set to 0
BL: register to set (color number)
BH: value of register (color — see table below)

**Function 1
Set overscan
register:**   Registers (set before function call):

Note: This function sets the border color. It only works properly when the EGA is in 200-line mode because the scan rate in 350-line mode is not high enough to cover the entire face of the screen.

AL: set to 1
BH: value of register (color)

**Function 2
Set all
palette
registers:**   Registers (set before function call):

Note: This function requires you to place a 17-byte table in memory. The first 16 bytes contain the values for palette registers 0–15, and the 17th byte contains the value for the overscan register.

AL: set to 2
ES: segment containing table
DX: offset of first byte in table

**Function 3
Toggle
intensify/
blink:**   Registers (set before function call):

AL: set to 3
BH: 0–enable intensify (disable blinking)
            1–enable blinking (disable intensify)

Register settings for the EGA and CGA

Color Display colors

7	6	5	4	3	2	1	0
X	X	X	I	X	R	G	B

ECD Colors

```
7  6  5  4  3  2  1  0
X  X  R' G' B' R  G  B
```

Default settings

Color	ECD	Color Display
Bit	5 4 3 2 1 0	5 4 3 2 1 0
Black	0 0 0 0 0 0	0 0 0 0 0 0
Blue	0 0 0 0 0 1	0 0 0 0 0 1
Green	0 0 0 0 1 0	0 0 0 0 1 0
Cyan	0 0 0 0 1 1	0 0 0 0 1 1
Red	0 0 0 1 0 0	0 0 0 1 0 0
Magenta	0 0 0 1 0 1	0 0 0 1 0 1
Brown	0 1 0 1 0 0	0 0 0 1 1 0
White	0 0 0 1 1 1	0 0 0 1 1 1
Dk. Gray	1 1 1 0 0 0	0 1 0 0 0 0
L. Blue	1 1 1 0 0 1	0 1 0 0 0 1
L. Green	1 1 1 0 1 0	0 1 0 0 1 0
L. Cyan	1 1 1 0 1 1	0 1 0 0 1 1
L. Red	1 1 1 1 0 0	0 1 0 1 0 0
L. Magenta	1 1 1 1 0 1	0 1 0 1 0 1
Yellow	1 1 1 1 1 0	0 1 0 1 1 0
I. White	1 1 1 1 1 1	0 1 0 1 1 1

The following functions are available on the VGA only:

Function 7
(VGA only)
Read Individual
Palette
Register: Registers (set before function call):

AL: set to 7
BL: register to read (color number)

Registers (read after function call):

BH: register setting

Function 8
(VGA only)
Read
Overscan
Register: Registers (set before function call):

AL: set to 8

Registers (read after function call):

BH: overscan setting

Function 9
(VGA only)
Read all
palette
registers: Registers (set before function call):

Note: This function requires you to reserve a
17-byte area in memory. After the call, the first 16 bytes
contain the values for palette registers 0-15 and the
17th byte contains the value for the overscan register.

AL: set to 9
ES: segment containing table
DX: offset of first byte in table

Function 10h
(VGA only)
Set Individual
DAC
Register: Registers (set before function call):

This function sets the 18-bit color value in the
designated DAC register. Each color should be a 6-bit
value.

AL: set to 10h
BX: DAC register to set (0-255)
CH: Green Intensity
CL: Blue Intensity
DH: Red Intensity

Function 12h
(VGA only)
Set Block
of DAC
Registers: Registers (set before function call):

This function sets the 18-bit color value for
multiple DAC registers. The program must place the settings in a table. The table contains sequential byte
values for the red, green, and blue registers, respectively
(3 bytes for each register programmed).

AL: set to 12h
BX: starting DAC register (0-255, typically 0)
CX: number of registers to program (1-256,
         typically 64 or 256).
ES: Segment of table
DX: Offset of table

Function 13h
(VGA only)
Select Color
Subset: Registers (set before function call):

This function sets the number of DAC subsets
available for 16 color modes (4 subsets of 16 colors, or 16
subsets of 16 colors). It is also used to select the active
subset.

AL: set to 13h
BL: 0 Select Paging Mode
BH: 0 4 sets of 64 DAC registers
         1 16 sets of 16 DAC registers
         1 Select Page
BH: Active DAC subset (0-3 or 0-15).

Function 15h
(VGA only)
Read Individual
DAC
Register: Registers (set before function call):

AL: set to 15h
BX: DAC register to read

Registers (read after function call):

CH:	Current Green Intensity
CL:	Current Blue Intensity
DH:	Current Red Intensity

Function 17h
(VGA only)
Read Block
of DAC
Registers: Registers (set before function call):

This function reads the 18-bit color value for
multiple DAC registers. The program must reserve 3
bytes of memory for each register read. After calling this
function, the table will contain sequential byte values
for the red, green, and blue registers, respectively.

AL:	set to 17h
BX:	starting DAC register (0-255, typically 0)
CX:	Number of registers to read (1-256, typically 64 or 256)
ES:	Offset of table location
DX:	Segment of table location

Function 1ah
(VGA only)
Read Color
Page State: Registers (set before function call):

This function returns the number of the active
DAC register subset, and the number of subsets available.

AL:	set to 1ah

Registers (read after function call):

BH:	Active subset number
BL:	0 4 sets available
	1 16 sets available

Function 1bh
(VGA only)
Sum DAC
Registers
to Gray
Shades: Registers (set before function call):

This function converts the designated block of
DAC registers to the equivalent shades of gray. Red becomes 30% of its current value; green, 59%; and blue,
11%.

AL: set to 1bh
BX: starting DAC register (0-255)
CX: number of registers to change (1-256).

Assembly Language Example:

This program prints a line of numbers across the
screen (one for each palette register). The numbers rep-
resent the current palette setting for each location. Starting on the right, the numbers are cycled, changing the
previous value when one completes a cycle (like an
odometer).

```
cry_f        equ     1                  ;carry flag emulation

data         segment public

clrs         db      16,15,14,13,12,11,10,9,8
             db      7,6,5,4,2,63,1,0

overscan     db      0
             flags   db          0

data         ends

code         segment public
             assume CS:code

main         proc    far

start:       push    DS
             sub     AX,AX
             push    AX
             mov     AX,data
             mov     DS,AX
             assume  DS:data
             mov     ES,AX
             assume  ES:data
             mov     AH,2       ;function 2 set cursor
             mov     DH,05      ;row 5
             mov     DL,0ah     ;column 10
             mov     BH,0       ;page 0
```

```
           int     10h            ;BIOS video call
           mov     CX,16          ;display each palette
                                  register

d_lp:      mov     BX,CX
           dec     BX             ;palette register number
           mov     AL,clrs [BX]   ;set the color
           call    show_new       ;display current value
           loop    d_lp
           mov     CX,1000h   ;number of color comb. to show
```

; If you set the initial colors all to 0, and used enough nested
; loops, this program would produce all possible palette combinations.
; Of course, it would take billions of millions of millenia to run. So,
; you might want to limit yourself to interesting initial values a few
; thousand iterations.

```
lp2:       push    CX
           mov     CX,16              ;check each palette reg
           or      flags,cry_f       ;set carry to add 1

lp1:       mov     BX,CX             ;put count in BX
           dec     BX                ;pal. reg. number
           mov     AL,clrs[BX]       ;get the color
           test    flags,cry_f       ;was carry set
           jz      no_c              ; no, do next pal. reg.
           inc     AX                ;faster than INC AL
           and     flags,not cry_f   ;change flag back to 0
           cmp     AL,64             ;is it maximum?
           jb      no_cry            ; no, don't carry
           sub     AL,AL             ;set color back to 0
           or      flags,cry_f       ;set carry flag

no_cry:    call    show_new          ;update the display
           mov     clrs[BX],AL       ;store the new color

no_c:      loop    lp1            ;check next palette reg.
           pop     CX             ;restore count
           loop    lp2            ;do next set

           ret

main       endp

show_new   proc    near

           push    AX             ;save current color
```

```
        push    BX          ;save current palette register
        push    CX          ;save current count
                            ;DX is destroyed
```

;Set the palette using option 0 (set one palette register) NOTE: you
; can also use option 2 by removing the 's from the "mov AL,2" and
; "mov DX,..." lines

```
        mov     BH,AL       ;BH=color, BL=palette register
        mov     AH,10h      ;function call 10h — set palette
        mov     AL,0        ;set one palette register
        mov     AL,2        ;set all palette regs.
        mov     DX,offset CLRS      ;point to color table
        int     10h         ;BIOS video call
        push    BX          ;save color/pal reg
        mov     AH,2        ;set cursor position
        mov     BH,0        ;page 0
        sub     DH,DH       ;DH=0 (row number)
        mov     DL,BL       ;put pal. reg. # in DL
        shl     DX,1
        shl     DX,1        ;col. number = 4*pal. reg. #
        int     10h         ;BIOS video call
        pop     BX          ;restore color/pal reg
        mov     AL,BH       ;put color back in AL
        call    bin2asc     ;convert AL to ASCII in AX
        push    AX          ;save AX
        xchg    AH,AL       ;put high digit in AL
        mov     AH,9        ;write attribute/character
        mov     BH,BL       ;put color number in BL
        mov     BH,0        ;page 0
        push    BX          ;save this for next digit
        mov     CX,1        ;write one character
        int     10h         ;BIOS video call
        mov     AH,2        ;set cursor position
        mov     BH,0        ;page 0
        inc     DX          ;next column
        int     10h         ;BIOS video call
        pop     BX          ;restore attribute and page
        pop     AX          ;restore color ASCII code
        mov     AH,9        ;write attribute/character
        int     10h         ;BIOS video call
        pop     CX
        pop     BX          ;restore current register
        pop     AX          ;restore color

        ret
```

```
show_new    endp

bin2asc     proc    near
```

COMMENT*   NOTE: unlike prior occurrences of this routine the
            equivalent AAM is used instead of DIV 10
            AL: 8 bit value to convert

            *

```
            aam                 ;AH=AL/10, AL=remainder
            add     AX,3030h    ;add 30h to get ASCII codes
            ret

bin2asc     endp

code        ends

end         start
```

Function Call 11h: Character Generator Functions

Remarks: This function manipulates and alters the character
            sets. Alpha modes allow up to four complete character
            sets (called blocks — there is one block for every 64K of
            memory installed on the EGA), although only two may
            be used at any one time, for a total of 512 usable charac-
            ters. Graphics modes allow only one character set of 256
            characters.

            This function also controls the number of display-
            able rows on the screen.

            Graphics character sets reside in the main system
            memory (either RAM or ROM). The alpha character sets
            reside in bit plane 2 of the EGA memory. However, the
            alpha sets must be loaded into the EGA from system
            RAM or ROM each time the mode is reset.

            Each row of each character consists of eight dots
            and uses one byte of memory (one bit per dot). The
            characters are arranged sequentially in memory start-
            ing with the top row of ASCII 0 and ending with the bot-
            tom row of ASCII 255 (see the table below). The alpha
            sets may consist of any contiguous segment, e.g., codes

25–32, but the graphics set must contain the entire set of 256 characters.

Note: The characters will return to the default set whenever the mode is reset. When using this function to change the character set, it should be used after every reset. Alternately, you may change the default set by modifying the BIOS SAVE_PTR table (a detailed description of this method appears in Chapter 12).

The 512-character set also reverts to a 256-character set when the mode is reset. In addition to modifying the BIOS SAVE_PTR, a new parameter table also needs to be built.

This function is usually the least compatible between manufacturers of various EGAs.

Input: Registers (set before function call):

AH: set to 11h

The following four functions will cause a mode reset. Display memory will not be affected, so the screen will look the same (with the exception of any characters which have been altered).

Function 0
User alpha
load: Registers (set before function call):

This function replaces the default set (or a portion of the set) with user defined characters.

AL: set to 0
BL: block to load (character set 0-3 [0-7 VGA])
BH: bytes per character (usually 8, 14, or 16)
CX: number of characters in table
DX: offset (ASCII code) of first character
ES: segment containing user character table
BP: offset of user character table

Function 1
ROM Mono-
chrome set: Registers (set before function call):

This function loads the ROM 14 row character set into one of the blocks.

AL: set to 1
BL: block number (character set 0-3 [0-7 VGA])

Function 2
ROM double
dot set: Registers (set before function call):

This function loads the ROM 8 row character set into one of the blocks.

AL: set to 2
BL: block number (character set 0-3 [0-7 VGA])

Function 3
Set block
specifier: Registers (set before function call):

This function creates a set of 512 characters in alpha mode (for systems with more than 64K EGA memory). It disables the intensity function of attribute bit 3 and replaces it with the alternate character set.

Since the character sets reside in bit plane 3, it is advisable to mask off bit plane 3 with attribute register 12h (the color plane enable register — see Chapter 4 for a description). This can be done through function call 10h (set AX to 1000h, BX to 0712h, and call INT 10h).

AL: set to 3
BL: bits 0–1, 4   block number for use when
              attribute bit 3 = 0
              bits 2–3, 5   block number for use when
              attribute bit 3 = 1

NOTE: bits 4 and 5 are used on the VGA only.

The following four functions should only be used after a mode reset. Page 0 must be active when these calls are initiated. Calling these functions causes a recalculation of the number of points (bytes per character), the number of character rows on the screen, and the length of the display buffer size in bytes. The following CRTC registers are also recalculated (see Chapter 4 for a description of the registers):

Register	Formula
9h*	points - 1
ah**	points - 2
bh	0
12h	(rows+1)*points - 1
	2*(rows+1)*points - 1
	[200 line VGA only]
14h***	points

* This register is calculated only for mode 7
** When the ECD is used with 14-row characters in alpha modes, this setting causes the cursor to disappear. This happens because the alpha modes always assume an eight-row character box for compatibility reasons (see function call 1).
*** This is a bug in the EGA ROM — the value should be points –1. This setting prevents the underline from appearing when the underline attribute is used.

**Function 4
ROM 16
row set:** Registers (set before function call):

This function loads the ROM 16 row character set into one of the blocks (VGA only).

AL: set to 4
BL: block number (character set 0-7)

**Function 10h
User alpha
load:** Registers (set before function call):

This function replaces the default set (or a portion of the set) with user defined characters.

AL: set to 10h
BL: block to load (character set 0-3 [0-7 VGA])
BH: bytes per character (usually 8, 14, or 16)
CX: number of characters in table
DX: offset (ASCII code) of first character
ES: segment containing user character table
BP: offset of user character table

Function 11h
ROM Monochrome
set: Registers (set before function call):

This function loads the ROM 14 row character set
into one of the blocks.

AL: set to 11h
BL: block number (character set 0-3 [0-7 VGA])

Function 12h
ROM double
dot set: Registers (set before function call):

This function loads the ROM eight-row character
set into one of the blocks.

AL: set to 12h
BL: block number (character set 0-3 [0-7 VGA])

**The following functions should only be used immediately
after a mode reset. These functions are designed for use in
graphics modes (the previous functions work only in alpha
modes).**

Function 14h
ROM 16
row set: Registers (set before function call):

This function loads the ROM 16-row character set
into one of the blocks (VGA only).

AL: set to 14h
BL: block number (character set 0-7)

The following functions should only be used
immediately after a mode reset. These functions are
designed for use in graphics modes (the previous functions work only in alpha modes).

Function 20h
User graphics
characters
(8 x 8):   Registers (set before function call):

This function sets INT 1fh to point to a table of
8 x 8 characters for ASCII codes 128–255. Its primary
purpose is for use in compatibility modes.

AL: set to 20h
ES: segment containing user character table
BP: offset of user character table

Function 21h
User graphics
characters: Registers (set before function call):

This function sets INT 43h to point to a table
of characters.

AL: set to 21h
BL: row specifier (character rows per screen)
       0–user defined (put number of rows in DL)
       1–14 rows
       2–25 rows
       3–43 rows
CX: points (bytes per character)
ES: segment containing user character table
BP: offset of user character table

Function 22h
ROM 8 x 14
set: Registers (set before function call):

This function sets INT 43h to point the ROM
table of 8 x 14 characters.

AL: set to 22h
BL: row specifier (character rows per screen)
       0–user defined (put number of rows in DL)
       1–14 rows
       2–25 rows
       3–43 rows

Function 23h
ROM 8 x 8
set: Registers (set before function call):

This function sets INT 43h to point the ROM
table of 8 x 8 characters.

AL: set to 23h

BL: row specifier (character rows per screen)
0–user defined (put number of rows in DL)
1–14 rows
2–25 rows
3–43 rows

Function 24h
ROM 8 x 16
set: Registers (set before function call):

This function sets INT 43h to point the ROM table of 8 x 16 characters.

AL: set to 24h

BL: row specifier (character rows per screen)
0–user defined (put number of rows in DL)
1–14 rows
2–25 rows
3–43 rows

The following function returns information about the character sets.

Function 30h
Information: Registers (set before function call):

AL: set to 30h

Registers (read after function call):

BH: 0 — return current INT 1fh setting
1 — return current INT 43h setting
2 — return ROM 8 x 14 character set location
3 — return ROM 8 x 8 character set location
4 — return upper half (starting at ASCII 128)
     ROM 8 x 8 character set location
5 — return ROM 9 x 14 alternate set location*
6 — return ROM 8 x 16 character set location
7 — return ROM 9 x 16 alternate set location*

CX: points (bytes per character)
DL: rows
ES: segment of returned location
BP: offset of returned location

* The monochrome adapter uses some characters which are shaped slightly differently than the ECD equivalents (such as the "M" and "$"). This table consists of the substitute characters for alpha mode 7. The 9 x 14 characters are defined as 8 x 8 characters. If the character is a block graphics code, the ninth column is the same as the eighth; otherwise, the ninth column is left blank.

Character Table Format:

ASCII 1

```
- - - - - - - -        0h
- - - - - - - -        0h
- X X X X X X -        7eh
X - - - - - - X        81h
X - X - - X - X        a5h
X - - - - - - X        81h
X - - - - - - X        81h
X - X X X X - X        bdh
X - - X X - - X        99h
X - - - - - - X        81h
- X X X X X X -        7eh
- - - - - - - -        0h
- - - - - - - -        0h
- - - - - - - -        0h
```

```
db      14 dup (0)                  ;ASCII 0
db      0,0,7eh,81h,a5h,81h,81h     ;ASCII 1
db      bdh,99h,81h,7eh,0h,0h,0h    ;ASCII 1
                                    ;ASCII 2 goes here
                                    ;ASCII 3 goes here
                                    ;etc.
```

Assembly Language Example:

The message "The quick brown fox jumps over the lazy dog" is printed, and the style of the letter "e" is changed to a small capital.

```
pause       macro
            local   no_adj, done
```

;this creates a processor independent approx. 10-second pause

```
                mov      AH,2ch        ;DOS get time call
                int      21h           ;DOS interrupt
                mov      BH,DH         ;put seconds in BH
                add      BH,10         ;add 10 seconds
                cmp      BH,60         ;if greater than 59, SUB 60
                jb       no_adj
                sub      BH,60

no_adj:         int 21h                ;DOS interrupt
                cmp      BH,DH
                je       done
                jmp      no_adj

done:
                endm

data            segment public

                msg      db            'The quick brown fox jumps
                                       over '
                         db            'the lazy dog.$'
                new_e    db            00000000b
                         db            00000000b
                         db            00000000b
                         db            00000000b
                         db            00000000b
                         db            00000000b
                         db            11111110b
                         db            10000000b
                         db            11111110b
                         db            10000000b
                         db            11111110b
                         db            00000000b
                         db            00000000b
                         db            00000000b

data            ends

code            segment public
                assume CS:code

main            proc     far

start:          push     DS
                sub      AX,AX
                push     AX
                mov      AX,data
```

```
        mov     DS,AX
        assume  DS:data
        mov     DX,offset msg       ;get the message address
        mov     AH,9                ;DOS print string call
        int     21h         ;DOS call

        pause

        mov     AX,1100h    ;User alpha load (& reset mode)
        mov     BL,0        ;character set 0
        mov     BH,14       ;14 bytes per character
        mov     CX,1        ;1 character
        mov     DX,65h      ;change the lowercase "e"
        push    DS
        pop     ES                  ;character in data seg.
        mov     BP,offset new_e     ;get offset of "e"
        int     10h                 ;BIOS video call

        pause

;set mode again to wipe out character set changes

        mov     AH,0        ;select function 0 set mode
        mov     AL,3        ;select mode 3
        int     10h         ;BIOS video call

        ret

main    endp

code    ends

end     start
```

Function Call 12h
Function
Call 12h: Alternate Select

Remarks: This function returns information about the adapter's
            current setting and provides an alternative print screen
            routine.

            The alternate print screen routine will print the
            entire screen when there are 43 rows (the standard
            print screen routine will print only 25 rows). It will not
            print graphics screens.

Input: Registers (set before function call):

     AH: set to 12h

Function 10h
Return
information: Registers (set before function call):

     BL: set to 10h

          Registers (read after function call):

     BH: 0 means a color mode is in effect (adapter
                registers are at port 3d?h)
                1 means a monochrome mode is in effect
                (adapter registers are at port 3b?h
     BL: Amount of memory installed on the
                adapter
                0 = 64K
                1 = 128K
                2 = 192K
                3 = 256K
     CH: Feature bit settings (see the description
                of the Feature Control register).
     CL: Switch settings (switches on the EGA card)

Function 20h
Select alternate
print screen
routine: Registers (set before function call):

          Calling this routine places the alternate print
          screen routine in effect.

     BL: set to 20h

**The VGA adds the following functions (AL will be set to 12h
after completion if the function is supported):**

Function 30h
(VGA only)
Select scan
lines for
alpha mode: Registers (set before function call):

Calling this routine changes the number of scan lines used the next time an alphanumeric mode is selected. This allows complete compatibility with MDA, CGA, and EGA display appearance.

BL: set to 30h
AL: 0 use 200 scan lines (CGA)
          1 use 350 scan lines (MDA and EGA)
          2 use 400 scan lines (VGA)

Output: Registers (read after function call):

AL: 12h

Function 31h
(VGA only)
Select Default
Palette
Loading: Registers (set before function call):

This function enables and disables the default palette during a mode reset. On the EGA, the default palette always overrides the current palette during a mode reset, but the VGA allows the current palette to remain.

BL: set to 31h
AL: 0 Enable the default palette
          1 Disable the default palette
          2 use 400 scan lines (VGA)

Output: Registers (read after function call):

AL: 12h

Function 32h
Video: Registers (set before function call):

This function enables and disables the adapter. When the adapter is disabled, the display will remain intact, but further reading and writing will have no effect until it is enabled.

BL: set to 32h
AL: 0 Enable the display
          1 Disable the display

Output: Registers (read after function call):

           AL: 12h

Function 33h
Summing
to Gray
Shades: Registers (set before function call):

           This function enables and disables color to gray
           scale conversion. When summing is enabled, the gray in-
           tensity is the sum of 30% red intensity, 59% green inten-
           sity, and 11% blue intensity after the next mode reset or
           when the palette registers are changed.

           BL: set to 33h
           AL: 0 Enable gray shade summing
                    1 Disable gray shade summing

Output: Registers (read after function call):

           AL: 12h

Function 34h
Cursor
Emulation: Registers (set before function call):

           This function enables and disables emulation of
           the CGA cursor in alphanumeric modes i.e. the cursor is
           set as if the character were only 8 pixels high (see the
           description of function call 1, Set Cursor Type). When
           emulation is disabled, the cursor setting reference ac-
           tual line numbers.

           BL: set to 34h
           AL: 0 Enable CGA cursor emulation
                    1 Disable CGA cursor emulation

Output: Registers (read after function call):

           AL: 12h

Function 35h
Display
Switch: Registers (set before function call):

This function toggles between the motherboard
adapter (VGA) and an external adapter if port and/or
memory addresses conflict. If an external adapter is
present, it will be the default adapter.

The first time displays are switched, the initiate
functions (AL=0 and AL=1) must be used. Thereafter, all
switching is accomplished through a double call: disable
the current active adapter (AL=2), then enable the current inactive adapter (AL=3). The program must provide
a 128 byte buffer for storing current state information
for each adapter.

BL: set to 35h
AL: 0 Initial external adapter off
        1 Initial VGA on
        2 Active Adapter Off
        3 Inactive Adapter On
ES: Segment of Switch State Area
DX: Offset of Switch State Area

Output: Registers (read after function call):

AL: 12h

Function 36h
Screen Off/On: Registers (set before function call):

This function turns the display on and off e.g.
screen blanking.

BL: set to 36h
AL: 0 Screen on (normal display)
        1 Screen off (blanked)

Output: Registers (read after function call):

AL: 12h

The presence test program in chapter 14 uses
alternate select.

Function Call 13h:	**Write String**

Remarks: This function writes a string of characters and attributes from memory to the screen. Two formats are available: the memory block can contain a sequential list of ASCII codes or an alternating list of character codes and attribute bytes. You may also choose whether or not the cursor moves to the end of the string or stays in the same location.

Note: The operation of this function call is similar to that of the teletype routine (eh). The bell, carriage return, and linefeed are treated as commands.

Input: Registers (set before function call):

AH: set to 13h
AL: bit 0 = 0: cursor not moved
bit 0 = 1: cursor moved
bit 1 = 0: string of characters only
bit 1 = 1: string of character, attribute, character, attribute, ...
BL: attribute (when AL bit 1 = 0)
BH: page number (see function call 5 for a description of pages)
CX: number of characters (do not include attribute bytes in this count).
DX: cursor location (DH = row, DL = column)
ES: segment containing string to be written
BP: offset of the first character in the string

Assembly Language Example:

This program prints a full string (message) at once. Note the effect of the control codes 7, 10, and 13. Compare the results to functions 9, ah, and eh.

```
data        segment public

            msg     db          'This line demonstrates
                                printing
```

```
                    db        'ASCII 7 (',7,'), 10 (',10,'), and'
                    db        ' 13 (',13,').'
        m_len       equ       $-msg   ;creates a constant from
                                      ;here to message start
                                      ;(message length)

data        ends

code        segment public
            assume CS:code

main        proc      far

start:      push      DS
            sub       AX,AX
            push      AX
            mov       AX,data
            mov       DS,AX
            assume    DS:data
            mov       AH,13h      ;function 13h — write string
            mov       AL,01b      ;character only, move cursor
            mov       BH,0        ;page 0
            mov       BL,15       ;attribute 15
            mov       CX,m_len    ;number of characters
            mov       DH,05       ;row 5
            mov       DL,0        ;column 0
            mov       BP,offset msg
                                  ;pointer to message
            push      DS
            pop       ES          ;message is in data segment
            int       10h         ;BIOS video call

            ret

main        endp

code        ends

end         start
```

Function Call 1ah: **Read/Write Display Combination Code (VGA only)**

Remarks: This function writes and returns codes designating the primary and secondary adapters. This is very useful for determining the display configuration, and will be supported on all future products. A result code is returned in register AL to confirm the operation of this function. If the result code is invalid, you can use alternate methods to determine the configuration (see the presence test program in Chapter 14 for an example program).

Input: Registers (set before function call):

AH: set to 1ah

Function 0
Read DCC: Registers (set before function call):

AL: set to 0

Output: Registers (read after function call):

AL: 1ah
BH: Secondary Display
BL: Active Display

Function 1
Write DCC: Registers (set before function call):

AL: set to 1
BH: Secondary Display
BL: Active Display

Output: Registers (read after function call):

AL: 1ah

DCC Code (BH/BL)	Meaning
0	No Display
1	MDA
2	CGA
4	EGA with standard color display

5	EGA with monochrome display
6	PGA (Professional Graphics Adapter)
7	VGA with analog monochrome display
8	VGA with analog color display
bh	MCGA with analog mono-chrome display
ch	MCGA with analog color display
ffh	Unknown

Function Call 1bh: **Return Functionality/State Information (VGA only)**

Remarks: This function returns information about the adapter/display environment. The same information may be found scattered throughout the BIOS Save Area and ROM data areas (see Chapter 12). However, the data is much easier to access through this function call. The program must allocate a 40h byte area for storing the returned information.

Input: Registers (set before function call):

AH:	set to 1bh
BX:	Implementation Type (set to 0)
ES:	Segment of the reserved storage area
DI:	Offset of the reserved storage area

Output: Registers (read after function call):

AL: 1bh

The table now located in ES:DI has the following structure:

Offset	Size	Description
0	1 word	Offset of Static Functionality Table
2	1 word	Segment of Static Functionality Table
4	1 byte	Current Video Mode
5	1 word	Number of Displayable

		Character Columns
7	1 word	Size of Video Data Area in Bytes
9	1 word	Starting Address in Video Data Area
bh	1 word	Page 0 Cursor Location
dh	1 word	Page 1 Cursor Location
fh	1 word	Page 2 Cursor Location
11h	1 word	Page 3 Cursor Location
13h	1 word	Page 4 Cursor Location
15h	1 word	Page 5 Cursor Location
17h	1 word	Page 6 Cursor Location
19h	1 word	Page 7 Cursor Location
1bh	1 byte	Cursor Starting Line
1ch	1 byte	Cursor Ending Line
1dh	1 byte	Current Display Page
1eh	1 word	CRTC Port Address
22h	1 byte	Number of Displayable Character Rows
23h	1 word	Character Pixel Height
25h	1 byte	Primary DCC (adapter)
26h	1 byte	Secondary DCC (adapter)
27h	1 word	Number of Colors Available
29h	1 byte	Number of Display Pages Available
2ah	1 byte	Number of Scan Lines:
		0–200 lines
		1–350 lines
		2–400 lines
		3–480 lines
2bh	1 byte	Primary Font Block Number (0–7)
2ch	1 byte	Secondary Font Block Number (0–7)
2dh	1 byte	Miscellaneous (stored in bits):

Bit	Description (when set to 1)
0	All Modes Available
1	Colors Summed to Gray Equivalents
2	Monochrome Display Attached
3	Default Palettes Not Loaded
4	Convert Cursor

			to CGA Equivalent
		5	Blinking (0=Background Intensity)
31h	1 byte	Video Memory (in 64K blocks, 0 = 64K)
32h	1 byte	Save Pointer Status (stored in bits):

Bit	Description (when set to 1)
0	512 Character Set in Use
1	Palette Save Area in Use
2	User Alpha Character Set in Use
3	User Graphics Character Set in Use
4	User Palette Set in Use
5	DCC Extension in Use

The Static Functionality Table (pointed to by the first four bytes) is 16 bytes long and has the following structure:

Offset	Size	Description
0	3 bytes	Video Modes Supported (1 bit per mode): 0,1,2,3,4,5,6,7,8,9,ah,bh,ch, dh,eh,fh 10h,11h,12h,13h,N/A,N/A, N/A,N/A
7	1 byte	Scan Lines Available in Alpha Mode:

Bit	Description (when set to 1)
0	200
1	350
2	400
8	1 byte Number of Alpha Mode Font Blocks
9	1 byte Number of Simultaneous

		Alpha Mode Font Blocks
ah	1 byte	Miscellaneous Functions Available:

Bit	Description (when set to 1)
0	All Modes Usable
1	Gray Shade Equivalents
2	User Defined Font Tables
3	User Defined Palette Tables
4	CGA Cursor Emulation
5	EGA Type Palette Registers
6	DAC Type Palette Registers
7	Multiple DAC Color Tables

bh	1 byte	Miscellaneous Functions Available:

Bit	Description (when set to 1)
0	Light Pen Interface
1	Save/Restore Video States
2	Background Intensity/Blinking
3	DCC Table

eh	1 byte	Save Pointer Functions Available:

Bit	Description (when set to 1):
0	512 Character Set
1	Palette Save Area
2	User Alpha Character Set
3	User Graphics Character Set
4	User Palette Set
5	DCC Extension

**Function
Call 1ch:**　　　　　**Save/Restore Video State**

Remarks:　This function returns saves (and restores) selected video environment parameters (BIOS, palette, and register settings). This saves a substantial amount of program overhead when the video mode must be changed, but current screen contents saved; e.g., memory resident software.

Note:　The program must reserve a data area to save the settings. The size of the area varies according to the parameters selected; function 0 returns the required size.

Input: Registers (set before function call):

                    AH: set to 1ch
                    CX: Selected Settings
                               Bit   Description
                               0   Video Hardware (registers)
                               1   BIOS RAM Data Area
                               2   DAC Registers

Function 0
Get Buffer
Size: Registers (set before function call):

                    AL: set to 0

Output: Registers (read after function call):

                    AL: 1ch
                    BX: Buffer Size Required (in 64K blocks)

Function 1
Save: Registers (set before function call):

                    AL: set to 1
                    ES: Segment of Save Area
                    BX: Offset of Save Area

Output: Registers (read after function call):

                    AL: 1ch

Function 2
Restore: Registers (set before function call):

                    AL: set to 2
                    ES: Segment of Restore Area
                    BX: Offset of Restore Area

Output: Registers (read after function call):

                    AL: 1ch

Now that you have had a chance to study the adapters and write some routines on your own, we will move on to new methods (and new functions not supported by BIOS). If you have written some BIOS-based plotting routines, you are probably very disappointed with their performance. Here is your chance to change that! If you've kept your code fairly clean with subroutines or macros for primitive operations, such as plotting, the conversion may go fairly smoothly. However, as you may be aware, the EGA and VGA are not particularly easy to program directly, so your first few tries may take quite some time. If you carefully study the example programs, you may greatly reduce the time and frustration. But before jumping right into the programs, you should understand how the EGA and VGA work.

5

Physical Construction

BIOS Calls vs. Direct Register and Memory Manipulation

Using BIOS calls is certainly easy, but many of the routines are painfully slow. Most programs write registers and memory directly in order to improve performance. Even with this direct interface to the hardware, many of the functions remain compatible between the CGA/monochrome and EGA/VGA systems. The primary exceptions are programs which aggressively program the CGA/monochrome 6845 registers (these correspond to the EGA/VGA CRTC registers). A few of the adapter's registers are significantly different from each other. Effective use of register programming and memory access requires a good understanding of the adapter's memory organization.

Direct Memory Manipulation

In alpha mode, memory locations are used to store the ASCII code of the character being displayed, as well as its attributes (color, intensity, and/or blinking). The first two bytes of memory on the adapter, as seen by the CPU, correspond to the character in the upper left corner of the screen, and the succeeding words (two bytes) correspond to the positions from left to right, going down the screen. The first byte of each word is the ASCII code of the character. The second byte is divided into groups of one and three bits, as shown in the following diagram.

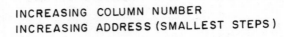

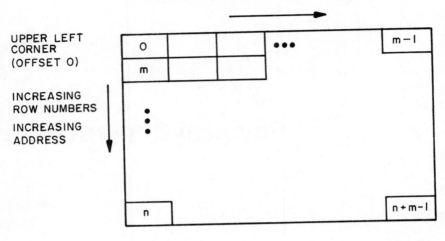

Figure 5-1 General memory/display correlation

| 7 | 6 | 5 | 4 | 3 | 2 | 1 | 0 |

| blink | background color | | | intensity | foreground color | | |

For color monitors, the three-color bits for background and foreground give eight colors. For monochrome monitors, the three background bits should be either all 0 (black) or all 1 (colored), and the three foreground bits should be set to one of the three values given in the table below (using other combinations may not give the same results on both the EGA and monochrome adapter). Memory locations begin at address b8000h for graphics monitors and b0000h for monochrome (nongraphics) monitors.

bit pattern	default colors	monochrome
000	black	black
001	blue	underline
010	green	
011	cyan	
100	red	
101	magenta	

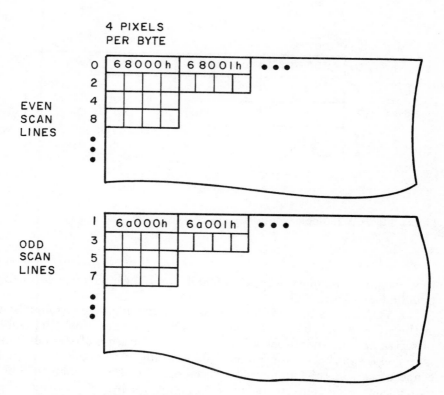

Figure 5-2 CGA two-color graphics

110	brown
111	white colored

In graphics mode, memory is used to store the colors for each pixel. The mapping of memory locations to pixel locations varies with the particular graphics mode in use and the amount of memory installed on the EGA (the VGA mappings are the same as the EGA with 256K installed memory). In all modes, the pixels are arranged left to right and top to bottom on the screen as the memory address increases (see Figure 5-1).

In *compatibility* modes, which work in the same manner as corresponding modes on the CGA, the display memory is interleaved. This means that there are two areas of memory for storing pixels — one area for the even-numbered rows and one area for the odd-numbered rows. Each byte contains information about several pixels, so it is more useful to refer to bits (hence the term "bit-mapped graphics"). In medium resolution, two bits refer to one pixel (giving four possible states and thus four colors), and in high resolution each bit is a single pixel (it can be on or off, thus giving two colors). The even-numbered

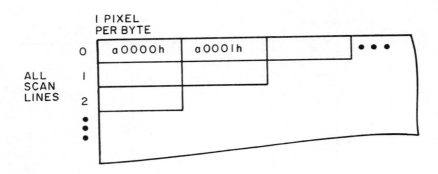

Figure 5-3 VGA 256-color mode

rows begin at memory location b8000h, and the odd rows begin at ba000h (see Figure 5-2).

The VGA adds a 320 x 200 mode, which resembles the organization of the CGA modes. This new mode uses one byte per pixel (the eight bits give 256 accessible colors) and a starting address of a0000h. The map is not split between even and odd scan lines; all pixels are stored consecutively as they appear on the screen. The one byte per pixel organization and continuous memory map makes calculating the memory address of each pixel very easy (see Figure 5-3).

The other new modes available on the EGA and VGA also use a much simpler map than the CGA, but writing different colors becomes more complicated. The starting address is a0000h for all of the new graphics modes. Each bit refers to one pixel, and thus each byte describes exactly eight pixels. You may wonder how up to 16 colors can be described with one bit, and the answer reveals an interesting feature of the EGA/VGA.

The memory is arranged in *bit planes*. Several planes can occupy the same address — for four color modes there are two planes, and for 16 color modes there are four planes. It is helpful to picture each plane as a bank of memory stacked upon another. At any single memory address, there are up to four bits — one from each plane (see Figure 5-4). Each possible combination of planes may designate a unique color (selected from 64 possibilities), and any combination of planes may be modified simultaneously.

A bit plane organization is convenient for three reasons. First, the location of a pixel on the screen corresponds exactly with its location in memory. And in the simplest case, each bit plane corresponds to a primary color and an intensity control (strictly speaking, this is not the case on the EGA and VGA, although it is true for the default color scheme). Second, the number of available colors can be doubled by

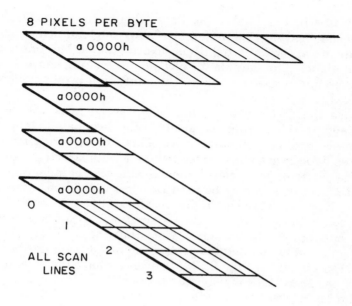

Figure 5-4 Bit plane organization

simply adding another bit plane. Programs which write directly to memory would not need to recalculate addresses for new, compatible adapters if additional colors would be added through new planes. Third, the memory can be modified as quickly in two-color mode as 1024-color mode (if such a mode were supported), since all planes can be modified with one memory access.

However, there is some additional processing required to handle bit planes. The additional planes would not be of much use if they all were written at once since you would still have only two colors. The adapter provides two methods for setting colored pixels from the CPU (a third method is available for moving data from one adapter memory location to another with all color data intact). The first method uses the *Map Mask register* to specify which bit planes should be set to 1. Each time you change the color, you must write the new value to the map mask register — much like selecting a new colored pen or crayon.

Note that the Map Mask register specifies which planes will *change*, not which planes will be set to 1. To write pure colors, you should write 0's to all planes (to clear the unmodified planes before writing). Alternatively, you could use the *Set/Reset* and *Enable Set/Reset* registers to clear the unmodified planes. First, write 0 to the Set/Reset register to write 0 to the enabled planes. Then use the logical negation of the Map Mask for the Enable Set/Reset register; i.e., if the Map

Mask is 0101b, the Enable/Set Reset should be 1010b. Using the Set/Reset method may be preferable for writing characters, since all eight bits are always affected (thus clearing the background); writing 0s to all planes is preferable for plotting (or writing characters with the background unaffected), since the unaffected pixel positions may be masked.

Because the CPU writes a full byte, each access will normally change eight pixels, turning on pixels in the designated planes where the bits are one, and off where zero. This can be handy for writing character data in graphics modes (where each character is an eight-bits-wide pattern), but does not allow the plotting of individual pixels. The *Bit Mask register* may be used to select individual pixels within the byte. Each bit set to one in the Bit Mask allows the corresponding bit in each byte to change — thus a single pixel can be modified by setting only one bit in the mask. Note that the pixel may either be turned on or off by making the corresponding CPU bit position either 1 or 0, respectively (i.e., the Bit Mask does not force the pixel to 1).

Using the Map Mask register to set colors is the BIOS default technique and is referred to as write mode 0 (not to be confused with the BIOS video modes). Since most BIOS functions work with character data, which come in 8-bit sets, it makes sense that BIOS would use such a technique. However, the EGA provides another method for writing video memory, which usually works better for plotting individual pixels. This method is called write mode 2 and may be set through the *Graphics Controller Mode register*. Write mode 2 does not require the use of the Map Mask register; the color number is placed in a CPU register and then written to the adapter's memory. This offers a significant advantage over write mode 0; with write mode 2, all four planes are written with 0 or 1 according to the selected color, saving one write (black before the color) or use of the Set/Reset registers. As with write mode 0, the pixels are selected with the Bit Mask register (write mode 2 is affected by the Map Mask register, which should normally be set to 0f to enable all planes).

Write modes 0 and 2 are also affected by other register settings. Of these, the *Data Rotate register* is used most frequently. The Data Rotate register sets the ALUs (Arithmetic Logic Units, internal devices which combine latch and CPU data for each plane) to perform logical functions between the CPU and adapter data. Thus, if you want to write text without affecting the background, you can AND an inverse image of the character with all bit planes and bits unmasked (to clear the pixels which form the character) and then OR the character pixels in the desired color (if it is something other than color 0). This technique is very useful for animation, too. Alternately, you could use the character pattern to set the bit mask and use write mode 2 to set the desired color directly from the processor.

On the surface, plotting may seem fairly easy to manage: (1) select the address and bit, (2) set the Map Mask register to 0f and write 0 to the address (unless using write mode 2), (3) set the color through the Map Mask register (unless using write mode 2), and (4) write the pixel. While this is essentially the correct outline, there are complications related to the hardware design, which make the task more difficult. For example, the CPU does not have direct access to the adapter memory. In order to preserve unmodified bits, the current adapter memory contents must be loaded into a set of *latch registers* (there are four 8-bit latch registers, one for each plane).

The latch registers are loaded by moving data from the adapter memory to the CPU; e.g., MOV AL,ES:BX where ES:BX points to the desired memory location (the value which appears in AL is usually ignored — it is affected by the read mode and is discussed later). When data is written from the CPU to memory, the CPU data is combined with the latch register data in the ALUs, and then stored in the adapter's memory. For the most part, this operation is transparent to the user, but several of the registers give you control over the process.

Additional hardware complications arise from the limited port address space of the PC family. For example, the Map Mask, Set/Reset, Enable Set/Reset, and Bit Mask registers are selected indirectly via address registers. The Map Mask register is accessed through the *Sequencer Address register*. The Sequencer Address register is written with the index of the Map Mask register, and then the Map Mask is written with the bit planes to modify. In this way, other registers can appear at the same port address as the Map Mask register to conserve address space. As with the bit planes which create "layers" of memory, you can think of this as layers of registers (although only one indexed register may be modified at any one time). The Bit Mask, Set Reset, and Enable Set/Reset registers are accessed in the same manner via the *Graphics 1 and 2 Address register*.

The EGA and VGA commonly use indirect reference for addressing registers (and memory, too), and it can become very confusing. In some cases, the references are three levels deep: an address points to a second address which points to a table of values. The following diagram may be helpful for picturing the register uses (the boldface register names are those mentioned above).

EGA registers used for accessing display memory and features are:

Sequencer Address	Reset
	Clocking Mode
	Map Mask
	Character Map Select
	Memory Mode Select
Graphics 1 and 2 Address	Set/Reset
	Enable Set/Reset
	Color Compare
	Data Rotate
	Read Map Select
	Mode
	Miscellaneous
	Color Don't Care
	Bit Mask

Let's go through a description of the plotting process to get a better understanding of its operation. We will assume the write mode is already set to 0, since this is the BIOS default. First, select the bit mask register through the Graphics 1 and 2 Address register. You will need to calculate the memory location of the pixel to change. Let's say you want to plot column 23 in row 183. With 640 pixels per row, this means you want to change bit 183 x 640 + 23 = 117,143. Now divide by 8 to get byte number 14,642 with a remainder of 7. At this point, the program could read the byte to load the latch register (we will assume DS points to the adapter segment).

```
mov    BX,14642    ; point to the byte
mov    AL,[BX]     ;  load the latch registers
```

The remainder of 7 indicates bit 0 needs to be set, since starting from bit 7 on the left and going right seven positions gets you to bit 0 (all orientation on the display is left to right). To modify bit 0 without affecting the other pixels in the byte, we need to set the bit mask register. To do this, select the Bit Mask by writing 8 to port 3ceh (the Graphics 1 and 2 Address register) and then writing 0, for bit 0, to port 3cfh (the Bit Mask register).

```
mov    DX,3ceh     ; select the Address register
mov    AL,8        ; index of the Bit Mask register
out    DX, AL
mov    DX, 3cfh    ; select the Bit Mask register
mov    AL,1        ; set the low bit of the Bit Mask
out    DX,AL
```

Next, select the Map Mask register through the Sequencer register. This is done by writing the value 2 to port 3c4h. Clear the current color by setting the mask to 0fh and writing 0. Then, the color value (which is simply a number representing the bit planes to be modified) is written to port 3c5h. Finally, the pixel can be set:

```
mov     DX,3c4h       ;point to the Sequencer Address register
mov     AL,2          ;index of the Map Mask register
out     DX,AL
mov     DX,3c5h       ;point to the Map Mask register
mov     AL,0fh        ;all bit planes (1111b)
out     DX,AL
mov     [BX],0        ; write 0 to clear the planes
                      ; note, the Map Mask is still in effect
mov     AL,0ah        ; color 10 — bit planes 4 and 2 (1010b)
out     DX,AL         ; set the Map Mask
mov     [BX],0ffh     ; write the color
```

This is a lot of code to do a simple operation like plotting a point (and the address calculations were not even included!). Of course, these fragments are not the most efficient — there are ways to reduce code size and increase the speed. A program that uses this method (write mode 0) to plot a multicolored line across the top of the screen can be found in Appendix A. The equivalent program using BIOS calls is listed under function call 0 in Chapter 2. The line and Ellipse programs demonstrate the use of write mode 2, which is much more appropriate for pixel plotting.

Methods for Storing and Manipulating Images

Reading and storing graphics images from the adapter is similar to writing. Again, either direct memory access or BIOS calls can be used. The large amount of memory required for a high resolution graphics page presents quite a storage problem. Each enhanced graphics image with 16 colors requires 110K bytes of memory for storage (154K for the VGA's highest resolution mode). Five screens would almost fill the free work space on a 640K PC. Also, the 110K of storage is larger than the 64K segment size on the 8086 family of processors. You should also be aware that the adapters can use a logical screen of up to 256K (64K in each of four bit planes), although only a portion will appear on the display. Two basic methods for reducing the required memory are data compression and vector representation. Before examining data compression methods, we will describe the various methods of reading data from the adapter.

Using BIOS calls for reading the display is much simpler than reading memory if speed is not critical. Interrupt 10h, function call 8 can be used to read characters in any mode and their associated attributes in alpha mode. Function call ch can be used to read the color of an individual pixel in graphics modes. Both of these function calls are described in the previous chapter.

Directly reading memory while the EGA is in the old modes is a simple task. In alpha modes, the odd addresses contain the character's ASCII code, and the following even address contains the attribute. In graphics modes, each bit represents a pixel being on or off in high resolution, or each group of two bits represents the color of a pixel in medium resolution. Remember that the display is interlaced — even and odd lines appear in different blocks of memory.

The bit plane arrangement of the new graphics modes makes reading the display memory more complicated. As was the case when writing to memory, the registers can be used to access the various bit planes. There are two methods for reading memory in the new modes. Read mode 0 uses the *Read Map Select register* to check a single bit plane; read mode 1 compares each address with a specific color in the *Color Compare register*.

Read mode 0 is the BIOS default method for reading memory. This is a three-fold process. First, the Read Map Select register is designated with the *Graphics 1 and 2 Address register*; this is done by writing its index, 4, to port 3ceh. Next, the number of the bit plane (0, 1, 2, or 3) that you want to read is written to the Read Map Select register at port 3cfh. Finally, you may read the EGA memory. Remember that you are examining only a single bit plane — you must repeat this process for each bit plane and combine the results to get the color number. This method is most effective when you only need the contents of any or all bit planes or when you want to reproduce the bit planes in the CPU's memory.

To use read mode 1, you must first select it (a two-step process). To do this, set the Graphics 1 and 2 Address register to point to the Mode register by writing 5 to port 3ceh. Then set read mode 1 by setting bit 4 of the mode register. Usually the other bits of the Mode register are set to 0 (although you should determine the current setting before changing it), and you would write 10h to port 3cfh (see the Mode register entry for a description of the settings).

When in read mode 1, you can test the color of a pixel against a single color of your choice by placing it in the Color Compare register. The Color Compare register is selected by writing 2 to port 3ceh (the Graphics 1 and 2 register). Next you write the color value to the Color Compare register at port 3ceh. Finally you read the EGA memory. You will see a set bit in every location where the display color matches the value in the Color Compare register. This method is very useful for scanning for a particular color or extracting only one color from the display. If you want to check for special blocks of colors, the Color Don't Care register can be set to ignore any or all of the bit planes (see Chapter 4). This mode is not very useful for getting the color of every pixel, because it requires 16 iterations (one for each color) as opposed to four iterations (one for each bit plane) for read mode 0. However it provides a convenient way to compress a graphics image into less memory.

Data Compression

Most graphics images can be compressed into a considerably smaller space than the bit maps use. It is not unusual for large stretches of sequential bits to be set to the same color. You can take advantage of this fact by storing a string of color values followed by a pixel count for that color. The following steps would work quite nicely:

1. Set the CPU's data address to the first display address.
2. Set the Color Compare register to 15 (or 0).
3. Read the first display address into a CPU register and check the high bit of the CPU register. If the bit is 0, select the next color and repeat this step.
4. Count the number of bits set to 1. All of the remaining bits are set to 1. Read the next byte. Continue counting bits until you find a 0, reach the maximum count (a 1-byte integer, 256, is probably best for most applications), or reach the end of the display.
5. Save the color and count, and return to step 2.

Be sure you don't overrun the allocated data area while using this algorithm.

If most of your images consist of recurring shapes, such as circles, lines, squares, and just a few points, you may want to store your image in tokenized form. Each basic shape is given an identification code followed by the relevant data (center and radius for a circle, endpoints for a line or square, coordinates for a point, etc.). Such images are easy to scale and do not use much memory. However, recreating the screen requires many calculations. Most CAD packages use this approach to store images.

Pages

For temporary storage, you may be able to use another page of memory. This works for all of the EGA modes (which support at least two pages), but all of the new VGA modes require too much memory to support a second page. A second page is ideal storage for complex backgrounds in animation packages. Rather than move an area which is about to be overwritten to a temporary storage area, you store its

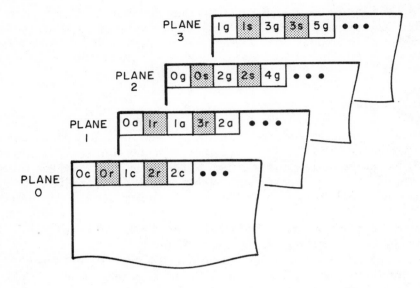

ACTUAL   MEMORY   LOCATIONS

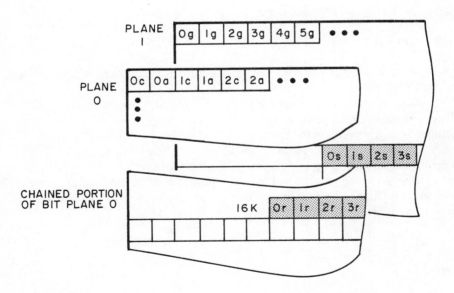

CPU   ADDRESSES

Figure 5-5 Memory chaining

coordinates (address). When the background needs to be restored, you simply copy the affected area from the second page to the first. The EGA and VGA even provide a method (write mode 1, see the Graphics Controller Mode register) for copying one byte of all four bit planes in one move.

Overview of EGA Construction

Normally, understanding the adapter's memory organization as seen by the CPU is sufficient for most programming applications. But if you will be changing to different video modes while preserving memory contents or making very heavy use of advanced register functions (especially those related to smooth scrolling), you should have a basic understanding of the adapter's techniques for reorganizing memory. In some cases, the adapter's view of memory is radically different from that of the CPU. The adapter uses several different mapping schemes, depending on the mode selected and the amount of memory installed.

In order to provide compatibility with the CGA modes, the adapter uses a method called odd/even address mode. In odd/even mode, odd memory addresses are written to odd bit planes and even addresses to even bit planes. Thus, b000:0000 is written to planes 0 and 2 and b000:0001 to planes 1 and 3. In alpha mode, this is used to send the ASCII code to plane 0 and the attribute code to plane 1. Figure 5-5 shows how this appears (the "c" represents a character, "a" attribute for alpha mode). This wastes memory, since the ASCII codes are stored only at the even CPU addresses and the attributes only at odd addresses. So, the adapter provides a second function, chaining odd maps to even maps. This function subtracts 1 from the odd CPU addresses (so that character and attribute data appear at the same adapter address on different planes) and doubles the address space by chaining the unused odd adapter addresses to the end of the even addresses.

While chaining is not terribly important for alpha mode, which uses very little memory, chaining can increase the number of available pixels in graphics mode (although it reduces the number of colors, since it effectively creates two-bit planes instead of four). This is why the original EGA is limited to four colors in 640 x 350 graphics when only 64K is installed.

The CGA graphics emulation essentially follows the same procedure as the alpha modes. However, instead of character/attribute data, the two planes hold sequential data bytes. To display the data, the adapter grabs two bytes of memory (one from each plane) for every eight-pixel section displayed. The Graphics Controller converts each pair of sequential bits (which form the CGA color) to parallel bits on planes 0 and 1 as they are sent to the Attribute Controller for display. The byte from plane 0 is converted first, and then the byte from plane 1.

6

Introduction to Register Programming

The EGA and VGA have several registers, which organize the adapters' housekeeping functions — we have already seen how some of the registers work. The adapter registers fall into five major groups, the External registers, the Sequencer registers, the CRTC (Cathode Ray Tube Controller) registers, the Graphics Controller registers, and Attribute registers. The five groups tend to have sets of closely related registers, although there are a few exceptions. The Sequencer controls memory access, timing, and data flow between the other registers, the CRTC controls timing related to the display, the Graphics Controllers primarily manage graphics mode functions, the Attribute Controller handles the color palette selections, and the External registers provide a few miscellaneous functions. The VGA adds a sixth set called the DAC (Digital to Analog Converter) which converts color numbers into voltages for the analog monitor.

As mentioned earlier, most of the registers are accessed indirectly. Each group (except for the External registers) has an address register. The address register is used to select the register to be modified. All of the nonaddress registers (except the External and Graphics Position registers) have an index. This index is written to the address register, and then the desired register is accessed. For example, to write the value 3 to the map mask register (index 2 of the Sequencer):

```
mov    DX,3c4h    ;Port number of the Sequencer Address
                   register
```

```
mov    AL,2        ;Index number of the Map Mask register
out    DX,AL
inc    DX          ;Port number of the Map Mask (3c5h)
mov    AL,3        ;Value we chose to write to the Map Mask
out    DX,AL
```

The EGA and VGA also have four latch registers, which are used during processor memory accesses. Each latch register (and a corresponding ALU) is associated with one of the bit planes. The latch registers are used to preserve some memory contents during a CPU write and report the memory contents during a CPU read, and the ALUs combine the CPU and latched data. For the most part, the latch registers and ALUs are transparent to the user and the CPU, but a few Graphics Controller Registers deal directly with the latch contents and control the ALU's operations. The most basic thing to remember is that the latch registers should be updated before every memory write. This is done simply by reading the contents of memory before writing a new value (just as in the CGA, where the old value is read into the CPU register, modified, and written back to memory). It is not necessary to use the value returned from the read; it simply is the technique whereby the latches are updated.

Whereas the latch registers and ALUs provide the interface between memory and the CPU, a set of four Shift registers (or Serializers) form the interface between the adapter and display. In normal graphics operation, each of the shift registers fetches a byte from display memory and then sends it one bit at a time to the Attribute Controller. The Attribute Controller uses the four bits (one from each Serializer) to select a color, form the palette, and, on the EGA, write the pixel to the display. On the VGA, the Attribute Controller passes an eight-bit value to the DAC (Digital to Analog Converter), which looks up the associated analog output voltage for the display.

Most of the EGA registers are write only (they cannot be read by the CPU). Any of the registers that are not write only are noted in the following sections. The VGA registers are read/write, except for the attribute address register, input status registers, and latch registers. A few of the VGA registers must be read and written at different port addresses: These are noted in the register descriptions.

All bits marked as "Not used" should be set to 0. If the adapter is a VGA, IBM recommends that the port be read, only the desired bits modified, and then write the result back to the port. This guarantees compatibility with future extensions to the EGA/VGA features.

Up to this point, all register programming examples have used the byte form of the OUT instruction (OUT DX,AL). Most configurations will allow the word form; i.e., OUT DX,AX where AL contains the index and AH is the value. A word OUT executes faster than two byte

OUTs, but will not work on a few hardware configurations. If you use word OUTs, you should be prepared to offer a modified version with byte OUTs — macros work very well for this (the SMOOTH.ASM program uses macros for this purpose). If your hardware does not support word OUTs, you may have to modify some of the remaining program examples.

You should also note that the Address register's index setting will remain in effect until changed (except for the Attribute registers). If you will be changing the same register repeatedly, you may be able to set the index outside the loop. Be aware that BIOS or hardware interrupt routines may change the index (you may want to temporarily disable interrupts while using this technique).

The External Registers

The External registers provide miscellaneous functions on the EGA and VGA. On the IBM EGA, these registers are not located on the VLSI chips (Attribute Controller, CRTC, Sequencer, and Graphics Controllers). These registers are called the General registers on the VGA, which contains all registers on a single chip. The External registers are directly written and read at their respective port locations. This differs from most of the VLSI registers, which are indirectly addressed through an indexing mechanism.

Port 3c2h: **Miscellaneous Output Register**

Description: This register provides several miscellaneous
functions.

Notes: A hardware reset forces all bits to 0.

This register is write-only on both the EGA and
VGA, although the VGA can read the setting from port
3cch.

Bits 2 and 3 (Clock Select) may be used to select
an external oscillator for the EGA's timing functions. By
attaching a faster clock to the feature connector, selecting it as a source, and adjusting the CRTC settings, you
can create higher resolution modes. However, your
adapter may not be able to tolerate the higher rate (it
could damage some chips), so such experimentation
should be done with extreme care. IBM specifies a maximum range of 14.3 to 28.4 MHz for the VGA.

BIOS Default Settings (all values are Hexadecimal):

Mode	0	1	2	3	4	5	6	7	d	e	f	10
	23	23	23	23	23	23	23	a6	23	23	a2	a7

Values for the Enhanced Color Display:

Mode	0	1	2	3
	a7	a7	a7	a7

Bits: 0   3b/3d CRTC I/O Address
                    This bit selects the port location of the CRTC
                    and Input Status 1 registers in order to
                    maintain compatibility with both the
                    monochrome and color display adapters. Setting
                    this bit to 1 selects 3b? (monochrome). A setting
                    of 1 selects 3d? (color).

         1   Enable RAM
                    Setting this bit to 0 disables the EGA
                    RAM from access by the CPU. A setting
                    of 1 (the normal setting) allows the CPU
                    to access EGA memory.

         2–3   Clock Select
                    The Sequencer Reset register should be used
                    to force a Synchronous Reset before changing
                    this register. These bits set the clock rate
                    according to the following table:

                    00b   14 MHz (from the bus)
                                 25 MHz VGA
                    01b   16 MHz (from the EGA board)
                                 28 MHz VGA
                    10b   External source (from the feature
                                 connector)
                    11b   Not Used

         4   Disable Internal Video Drivers
                    (EGA Only)
                    This bit selects the signal source for the
                    monitor. Normally, this bit is set to 0 and the
                    EGA drives the monitor. When set to 1, the
                    monitor is driven by the signal output pins of
                    the feature connector. Since the feature
                    connector also provides signal input pins, a
                    device could be built which combines video

information from the EGA and another source
and then directly drives the EGA monitor.
This bit is not used on the VGA.

5   Page Bit for Odd/Even
This bit selects between the two 64K pages of
memory (of a 128K plane) when the EGA is in
Odd/Even mode. A setting of 0 designates the
low page, and 1 designates the high page.

6   Horizontal Retrace Polarity
The horizontal retrace signal is positive when
this bit is 0 and negative when 1. The
monochrome, color, and enhanced color displays
use a positive signal. The analog monitors use
this bit (and bit 7) to determine the scan rate.

7   Vertical Retrace Polarity
The vertical retrace signal is positive when this
bit is 0 and negative when 1. The monochrome
and monitor requires a negative signal, the
standard color monitor requires a positive
signal, and the ECD and analog monitors use
this bit (and bit 6) to determine the scan rate.

Bits 6 and 7	EGA	VGA
00b	200 lines	Not used
01b	350 lines	350 lines
10b	Not used	400 lines
11b	Not used	480 lines

Port 3?ah: **Feature Control Register**

Description: On the EGA, these bits send signals to the feature
connector (lines FC0 and FC1). Thus, a device attached
to the feature connector may be placed under program
control — the function would be defined by the attached
device.

The port address is either 3bah (monochrome) or
3dah (color).

Notes: The VGA reserves the use of all 7 bits, and bit 3
must be set to 0.

This is a write only register on both the EGA and VGA, although the value may be read from port 3cah of the VGA.

Bits: EGA only:

0   Feature Control Bit 0 (FC0)
             This bit is output from the CPU to pin 21 of the feature connector.

1   Feature Control Bit 1 (FC1)
             This bit is output from the CPU to pin 20 of the feature connector.

2–3   Reserved

6–7   Not used

             VGA only:

0–7   Reserved (bit 3 must be set to 0).

Port 3c2h: Input Status Register Zero

Description: This register allows the CPU to read various information from the EGA.

Notes: This register is read-only on both the EGA and VGA.

             On the EGA, bits 5 and 6 receive signals from the feature connector (lines FEAT 0 and FEAT 1). Thus, a device attached to the feature connector may send information to the controlling program — the meaning would be defined by the attached device.

             Bits 5 and 6 are reserved on the VGA.

             Some early model EGA compatibles have bit 7 backwards (0 indicates a vertical interrupt). Programs which rely on a vertical interrupt handler should determine which setting is used by disabling the vertical retrace interrupt, clearing the status bit (see bit 4 of the

CRTC Vertical Retrace End register, port 3?5h index 11h), reading bit 7 to get the value for no retrace, and re-enabling interrupts. This method should be used only on the EGA.

Bits: 0–3   Unused

4   Switch Sense
This bit returns the setting of one of the four switches on the EGA. If it is set to 1 the switch is open, 0 is closed. The switch to read is selected by writing the switch number minus one to bits 2 and 3 of the Miscellaneous Output register (also port 3c2h). For example, sending 9 (1001b) to the Miscellaneous Output register would return the setting of switch 3 to this bit. BIOS uses this bit to determine the EGA settings, which are then recorded at memory address 40:88h. Your code should not need to access the switches through this register.

5   Feature Code Bit 0 (FEAT 0 — EGA only)
This bit is input from pin 19 of the feature connector to the CPU.

6   Feature Code Bit 1 (FEAT 1 — EGA only)
This bit is input from pin 17 of the feature connector to the CPU.

7   CRT Interrupt
This bit is set to 1 when a vertical interrupt (IRQ2) has occurred because of the vertical retrace. It will remain set to 1 until cleared, and thus it is important that the interrupt handler clear and then reenable the interrupt via the CRTC's Vertical Retrace End register. It is used to confirm that the interrupt was enabled by the EGA or VGA, since several devices may share the IRQ2 line. This bit should be cleared to 0 by the interrupt handler (see bit 4 of the CRTC Vertical Retrace End register, port 3?5h index 11h).

Port 3?ah: Input Status Register One

Description: This register allows the CPU to read various
information from the adapter.

The port address is either 3bah (monochrome) or
3dah (color).

Notes: This register is read-only on both the EGA
and VGA.

Bits 1 and 2 are reserved on the VGA.

Bits: 0   Display Enable
This bit is set to 1 during the active display
interval (memory is being read by the EGA).
It is set to 0 during the vertical and horizontal
retrace. Some graphics adapters (such as the
CGA) may produce snow if the CPU writes to
adapter memory during the display interval due
to conflicts between CPU and adapter memory
access. However, EGA memory may be written
by the CPU at any time (see bit one of the
Sequencer Clocking Mode register, port 3c5h
index 1).

1   Light Pen Strobe (EGA only)
This bit is set to 1 when the light pen trigger
has been set (it is 0 when the light pen trigger
has not been set).

2   Light Pen Switch (EGA only)
This bit is set to 1 when the light pen switch
is open (it is 0 when the light pen switch
is closed).

3   Vertical Retrace
This bit is set to 1 during the vertical retrace
interval (it is set to 0 when the interval ends
and until it begins again). This bit can be used
to enable the IRQ2 interrupt (see the CRTC
Vertical Retrace End register, port 3?5h index
11h; and bit 7 of the Input Status Register
Zero, port 3c2h). Note that this bit will also be
set to 1 if the EGA IRQ2 is enabled and
another device issues an IRQ2 — it should not

be used to determine the status of the vertical
retrace in interrupt routines (see bit 7 of Input
Status Register Zero).

4–5   Diagnostic Usage
       These bits return the settings of two of the
       Attribute register output bits. The two which
       appear are selected via bits 4 and 5 of the
       Attribute Color Plane Enable register
       (see port 3cfh index 12h of the Attribute
       registers).

6–7   Not used.

Port 3c3h: Video Subsystem Enable Register (VGA only)

Description: This register controls the activity of the VGA.
The VGA memory and ports may be disabled via the
VGA sleep bit (bit 1 of port 102h). When the VGA is disabled, it may continue to generate an image on the attached monitor if bit 0 of this register is set to 1.

Notes: This register may still be accessed when the VGA
           is in sleep mode, and thus the display image may be
           turned on or off at any time via program control.

Bits: 0   Setting this bit to 1 enables the VGA
                   display (a setting of 0 disables the display).

           1–7   Reserved

7

The Sequencer Registers

The Sequencer's primary task is to control the data flow from memory or the Graphics Controller to the Attribute Controller. On every dot clock during the display interval, the Attribute Controller must have four bits to convert into a colored pixel. In graphics mode, a byte of data is fetched from each bit plane on every character clock. In the simplest case, it is then converted to individual bits in four streams (one from each plane) for use by the Attribute Controller. In alpha mode, the ASCII character code must be converted into the corresponding bit streams for the current scan line, while the attribute byte modifies the four bit streams to give the appropriate foreground and background color. On the EGA, the Attribute Controller output directly controls the display. The VGA uses the output of the Attribute Controller to look up colors in the DAC, which then outputs an analog signal to the monitor.

The Sequencer controls the dot clock, flow of the bit streams, and location of the alpha mode character generator. It also arbitrates memory access between the CPU and adapter and controls which bit planes may be modified by the CPU. The Map Mask register and Character Map Select register (along with the Sequencer Address register) are probably the only registers from this group that you will ever use (unless you design your own video modes).

Port 3c4h: Sequencer Address Register

Description: The Sequencer Address register selects which register will appear at port 3c5h. The index number of the desired register is written to port 3c5h.

Index   Register

0   Reset
1   Clocking Mode
2   Map Mask
3   Character Map Select
4   Memory Mode

Port 3c5h: Reset Register (Index 0)

Description: This register is used to reset the sequencer (necessary for preserving the contents of EGA memory when the Clocking Mode register is changed).

Notes: Both bits 0 and 1 must be set to 1 for the Sequencer to run.

BIOS Default Settings (all values are Hexadecimal):

Mode	0	1	2	3	4	5	6	7	d	e	f	10
	03	03	03	03	03	03	03	03	03	03	03	03

Bits   0   Asynchronous Clear
                         A value of 0 causes an asynchronous clear and halt of the sequencer register and places all outputs in a high impedance state. This may also result in data loss.

             1   Synchronous Clear
                         A value of 0 causes a synchronous clear and halt of the sequencer register. This is the bit that should be used to reset the Sequencer prior to changing the Clocking Mode register (see index 1) or the clock select function of the Miscellaneous Output register (see port 3c2h of the External registers).

             2–7   Not used

Port 3c5h: Clocking Mode Register (Index 1)

Description: The Clocking Mode register controls some of the timing functions of the EGA. To prevent changing the adapter's memory, you should use the Reset register to force a synchronous reset of the Sequencer before changing the clocking mode.

BIOS Default Settings (all values are Hexadecimal):

Mode	0	1	2	3	4	5	6	7	d	e	f	10
	0b	0b	01	01	0b	0b	01	00	0b	01	05	05

More than 64K EGA memory:

Mode	f	10
	01	01

Bits	0	8/9 Dot Clocks

Setting this bit to 1 generates a standard, 8-bit-wide character box (i.e., 8 dot clocks per character clock). 0 generates a 9- bit-wide character box for mode 7 MDA compatibility and VGA text modes (all other modes must use an 8-bit-wide character box). Note that the VGA may also emulate EGA or CGA text modes, in which case it uses an 8-bit-wide character

1   Bandwidth (EGA only)
This bit controls memory access time for the CRT. A setting of 1 gives the CRT 2 of every 5 memory access cycles. A setting of 0 gives the CRT 4 of every 5 cycles. Because higher resolution modes require more data during a horizontal scan, all modes except 0, 1, 4, 5, and 0dh require 4 out of 5 cycles for the CRT refresh. This directly affects the wait states generated by the adapter. The CRT continues to use cycles even during the retrace periods (the VGA gives the CPU full access during the retrace).

2   Shift Load

The shift registers serialize data from the bit planes for use by the attribute controller. Normally, 8 bits from each plane are converted into a serial bit stream. Setting shift load to 1 combines the data from two planes as a 16-bit serial stream, but now instead of four streams there are only two, halving the number of available colors and doubling the linear address space. Since two bytes are fetched at once, this mode only accesses adapter memory every other character clock. Also see the Graphics Mode register (index 5 of the Graphics Controller).

3   Dot Clock

Setting this bit to 1 divides the dot clock by 2 (half as many dots per line). This doubles those time intervals based on the dot clock to support 320 x 200 pixel and 40-column character modes. A setting of 0 does not alter the dot clock.

4   Shift 4 (VGA only)

This is similar to bit 2 of this register, except that a setting of 1 selects a four-word address and loads the serializers every fourth character clock (32 bits are chained and the linear address space is quadrupled). None of the VGA's internal modes use this setting, since there is plenty of memory for all programmed modes.

5   Screen Off

Setting this bit to 1 disables the display while the internal adapter functions continue to operate. This may be used to temporarily assign all memory access time to the CPU in order to rapidly fill or read the adapter memory (it would also be useful for a VGA screen blanking program)

6–7   Not used

Port 3c5h: Map Mask Register (Index 2)

Description: The Map Mask register enables or disables the specified bit planes during a memory write. Each bit set will allow that bit plane to be modified; e.g., setting bits 1 and 3 allows the CPU to write data to bit planes 1 and 3.

Notes: When using odd/even modes, bits 0 and 1, and 2 and 3 should have the same value. See the Graphics Controller Mode register (port 3cfh, index 5), and the Sequencer Memory Mode register (index 4). When using Chain 4 mode, all four maps should be set the same.

This register affects all write modes, i.e., all data written to adapter memory.

BIOS Default Settings (all values are Hexadecimal):

Mode	0	1	2	3	4	5	6	7	d	e	f	10
	03	03	03	03	03	03	01	03	0f	0f	0f	0f

Bits:	0	Bit plane 0
	1	Bit plane 1
	2	Bit plane 2
	3	Bit plane 3
	4–7	Not used

Port 3c5h: Character Map Select Register (Index 3)

Description: This register selects which section of bit plane 2 contains the character generator(s) in alphanumeric modes. Bit plane 2 is divided into 1-4 8K sections (depending on the amount of memory installed on the EGA). On the EGA, each of these sections may contain one character generator for a total of four. The VGA allows each section to hold two character maps. Two of these four (or eight) may be selected as the primary and secondary character sets for a total of 512 displayable characters (chosen from a possible 1024 or 2048). The

EGA supports 256 character definitions for every 64K installed.

Notes: Usually, character map A and B have the same value and only 256 characters are available. However, when maps A and B are programmed with different values, attribute bit 3 (intensity) is used as the character set selector (and what appears as high intensity in most programs will appear as the additional 256 characters).

The EGA must have more than 64K installed to enable this function.

The Character Map Select register should be set only after the sequencer is reset (an asynchronous reset clears this register to 0).

BIOS Default Settings (all values are Hexadecimal):

Mode	0	1	2	3	4	5	6	7	d	e	f	10
	00	00	00	00	00	00	00	00	00	00	00	00

Bits 0–1 Character Map Select A
This binary value selects the 8K section used for the primary character set (attribute bit 3 = 0). A value of 0–3 selects banks 0–3, respectively.

2–3 Character Map Select B
This binary value selects the 8K section used for the secondary character set (attribute bit 3 = 1). A value of 0–3 selects banks 0–3 respectively.

4 Character Map Select High Bit B (VGA Only)
This adds an extra bit to the secondary character set number, for a total of eight possible locations.

5 Character Map Select High Bit A (VGA Only)
This adds an extra bit to the primary character set number, for a total of eight possible locations.

6–7   Not used

Port 3c5h: Memory Mode Register (Index 4)

Description: This register controls the sequencer mode settings.
See the Graphics Controller Mode and Miscellaneous
registers for the Graphics Controller mode settings, and
the CRTC Mode Control register for the CRTC mode settings.

BIOS Default Settings (all values are Hexadecimal):

Mode	0	1	2	3	4	5	6	7	d	e	f	10
	03	03	03	03	02	02	06	03	06	06	00	00

More than 64K EGA memory:

Mode	f	10
	06	06

Bits: 0   Alpha (EGA only)
                        This bit is set to 1 for alphanumeric modes
                        and 0 for graphics modes. Alpha mode enables
                        bit plane 2 as the character generator.

             1   Extended Memory
                        This bit is set to 1 to enable address bit 14
                        and 15 when more than 64K of memory is
                        installed on the adapter. A setting of 0 should
                        be used for high resolution modes on the EGA
                        when no memory expansion card is installed.

             2   Odd/Even Mode
                        When this bit is set to 0, CPU data at odd
                        addresses is mapped to the odd bit planes
                        (and even addresses to even bit planes). This
                        only affects the Sequencer. Typically, the
                        Graphics Controller is set to use the same
                        scheme through bit 4 of the Graphics
                        Controller Mode register (see port 3cfh, index 5).
                        This is useful for alphanumeric modes
                        (attribute data in one plane, character data
                        in the other), emulating CGA graphics modes,

or addressing two bit planes as one when less than 64K is available.

3 Chain 4 (VGA only)
This is similar to odd/even modes, except that it forms a cycle of four rather than two. Mod 0 CPU addresses map to plane 0, mod 1 to plane 1, mod 2 to plane 2, and mod 3 to plane 3. A setting of 1 selects Chain 4 (used for 256 color mode). Each bit plane holds every fourth byte although the CPU sees them as a single plane of contiguous memory.

4–7 Not used

8

The CRT Controller Registers

The CRTC (Cathode Ray Tube Controller) registers form the largest register group on the EGA and VGA. As their names imply, these registers control the monitor (CRT) timing and synchronization functions. The CRTC registers are unique in that they may appear at either one of two port addresses: 3b4h/3b5h (for monochrome displays) or 3d4h/3d5h (for color displays). Most of these registers replicate the functions of the 6845 controller found on the MDA and CGA, although there are a few minor differences. When the EGA was introduced, several CGA programs would not run in emulation mode on the EGA because of the differences.

Most incompatibilities result from programs which support composite monitors. On composite monitors, images could be centered via the Horizontal Sync Position register (port 3d5h index 2). However, the EGA does not support composite monitors, and index 2 is used as the Start Horizontal Blanking register. The following table summarizes the differences:

Port 3d4h

Index	CGA/MDA	EGA/VGA
2	Horizontal Sync Position	Start Horizontal Blanking
3	Horizontal Sync Width	End Horizontal Blanking
4	Vertical Total	Start Horizontal Retrace
5	Vertical Total Adjust	End Horizontal Retrace
6	Vertical Displayed	Vertical Total
7	Vertical Sync	PositionOverflow
8	Interlace Mode	Preset Row Scan

Also, ports 3d8h (Mode Select register) and 3d9h (Color Select register) are not used by the EGA or VGA. Some CGA programs use 3d8h to disable blinking and 3d9h to change the foreground color for 640 x 200 graphics.

Port 3?4h: CRTC Address Register

Description: The CRTC Address register selects which register will appear at port 3b5h (for monochrome displays) or port 3d5h (for color displays). The index number of the desired register is written to port 3b5h or 3d5h.

Index   Register

0	Horizontal Total
1	Horizontal Display End
2	Start Horizontal Blanking
3	End Horizontal Blanking
4	Start Horizontal Retrace
5	End Horizontal Retrace
6	Vertical Total
7	Overflow
8	Preset Row Scan
9	Max Scan Line
ah	Cursor Start
bh	Cursor End
ch	Start Address High
dh	Start Address Low
eh	Cursor Location High
fh	Cursor Location Low
10h	Vertical Retrace Start (write [EGA], read/write [VGA])
10h	Light Pen High (read, EGA only)
11h	Vertical Retrace End (write [EGA], read/write [VGA])
11h	Light Pen Low (read, EGA only)
12h	Vertical Display End
13h	Offset
14h	Underline Location
15h	Start Vertical Blanking
16h	End Vertical Blanking
17h	Mode Control
18h	Line Compare

Note: Bit 5 is used for chip testing on the VGA — it should always be set to 0.

Port 3?5h: Horizontal Total Register (Index 0)

Description: This register is programmed with the number of character widths in the horizontal scan, plus the period of the horizontal retrace (this may be either the end of the horizontal blanking for compatibility modes or the end of the horizontal retrace for the EGA modes).

An internal counter resets after reaching the value programmed into the Horizontal Total register. The internal counter is the basis for all CRT timings. The new interval begins one count after the end of the prior interval.

Notes: The value used by the horizontal total register is actually two less than the total number of character widths on the EGA, and five less on the VGA.

The adapter always counts the first displayable position as the first scan count. The next intervals include the right overscan, horizontal blanking, and finally the left overscan. Timing constraints require that the adapter end the retrace count before ending the horizontal blanking. Thus, the retrace ends before the blanking and causes border colors to appear on the left edge of the displayable area if the border color is not black.

This register also controls the horizontal pixel size. The full count must occur within the total horizontal scan and retrace, and thus a higher value produces a smaller horizontal pixel size.

BIOS Default Settings (all values are Hexadecimal):

Mode	0	1	2	3	4	5	6	7	d	e	f	10
	37	37	70	70	37	37	70	60	37	70	60	5b

More than 64K EGA memory:

Mode	f	10
	60	5b

Values for the Enhanced Color Display:

Mode   0   1   2   3
      2d 2d 5b 5b

Bits: 0—7   Character count (minus two for the
                        EGA/minus five for the VGA) of the full horizontal cycle
                        time.

**Port 3?5h: Horizontal Display Enable End Register
                 (Index 1)**

Description: This register is programmed with the number of
             character widths in the displayable area. After the inter-
             nal counter reaches the Horizontal Display Enable End
             value, the overscan begins.

Notes: The value used by the Horizontal Display Enable
             End register is actually 1 less than the total number of
             character widths (so that a value of zero designates one
             character).

             The adapter always counts the first displayable
             position as the first scan count. The next intervals in-
             clude the right overscan, horizontal blanking and
             retrace, and finally the left overscan.

BIOS Default Settings (all values are Hexadecimal):

Mode 0   1   2   3   4   5   6   7   d   e   f   10
     27   27   4f   4f   27   27   4f   4f   27   4f   4f   4f

Bits: 0–7   Character count (minus one) of the
                        displayable screen width — usually 39 or 79.

Port 3?5h: Start Horizontal Blanking Register (Index 2)

Description: This register is programmed with the count value
             at which horizontal blanking signal becomes active (this
             is based on the internal counter which starts with 0 and
             ends with the value in the Horizontal Total register).
             The right overscan ends after the internal counter
             reaches the Start Horizontal Blanking value.

Notes: The adapter always counts the first displayable position as the first scan count. The next intervals include the right overscan, horizontal blanking and retrace, and finally the left overscan.

During the horizontal blanking interval, the address for the next scan line and underline position appear on the memory address and cursor outputs, and remain until one count after the end of the interval.

BIOS Default Settings (all values are Hexadecimal):

Mode	0	1	2	3	4	5	6	7	d	e	f	10
	2d	2d	5c	5c	2d	2d	59	56	2d	59	56	53

Values for the Enhanced Color Display:

Mode	0	1	2	3
	2b	2b	53	53

Bits: 0–7 Character count at which the Horizontal Blanking interval begins.

Port 3?5h: End Horizontal Blanking Register (Index 3)

Description: This register is programmed with the five least significant bits of the count value at which horizontal blanking signal becomes inactive (this is based on the internal counter which starts with 0 and ends with the value in the Horizontal Total register). The right overscan ends after the internal counter reaches the Start Horizontal Blanking value.

This register also provides a skew control which delays the start of the displayable area after the Horizontal Total has been reached. This allows the CRTC to access the character and attribute data, the character generator (bit plane 2), and Horizontal Pel Panning register (see the Attribute Controller registers) in order to convert ASCII data into bit stream data.

The skew control synchronizes the beginning of the displayable area with the start of the internal count. If the skew is set too low, the leftmost character will appear more than once; if too high, one or more characters may disappear.

Notes: The most significant bits of the End Horizontal
          Blanking count are always assumed identical to the
          most significant bits of the Start Horizontal Blanking
          register.

          The adapter always counts the first displayable
          position as the first scan count. The next intervals in-
          clude the right overscan, horizontal blanking and
          retrace, and finally the left overscan.

          During the horizontal blanking interval, the
          address for the next scan line and underline position ap-
          pear on the memory address and cursor outputs, and
          remain until one count after the end of the interval.

BIOS Default Settings (all values are Hexadecimal):

Mode	0	1	2	3	4	5	6	7	d	e	f	10
	37	37	2f	2f	37	37	2d	3a	37	2d	1a	17

More than 64K EGA memory:

Mode	f	10
	3a	37

Values for the Enhanced Color Display:

Mode	0	1	2	3
	2d	2d	37	37

Bits: 0–4   Character count at which the Horizontal
                    Blanking interval ends. The VGA uses a sixth
                    bit which is located in the End Horizontal
                    Retrace register (index 5).

          5–6   00b — No delay
                    01b — Delay of 1 character
                    10b — Delay of 2 characters
                    11b — Delay of 3 characters

          7   Unused on the EGA.
                    Used for chip testing on the VGA, and should
                    always be set to 1.

Port 3?5h: **Start Horizontal Retrace Pulse Register (Index 4)**

Description: This register is programmed with the count value at which horizontal retrace pulse becomes active (this is based on the internal counter which starts with 0 and ends with the value in the Horizontal Total register). This initiates the beam's move to the left of the screen. The timing of the horizontal retrace is responsible for screen centering.

Notes: The adapter always counts the first displayable position as the first scan count. The next intervals include the right overscan, horizontal blanking and retrace, and finally the left overscan.

                 The horizontal retrace may be delayed through the End Horizontal Retrace register.

BIOS Default Settings (all values are Hexadecimal):

Mode	0	1	2	3	4	5	6	7	d	e	f	10
	31	31	5f	5f	30	30	5e	51	30	5e	50	50

More than 64K EGA memory:

Mode	f	10
	50	52

Values for the Enhanced Color Display:

Mode	0	1	2	3
	28	28	51	51

Bits: 0–7   Character count at which the Horizontal Retrace begins.

Port 3?5h: **End Horizontal Retrace Register (Index 5)**

Description: The End Horizontal Retrace register is programmed with the five least significant bits of the count value at which horizontal retrace signal becomes inactive (based on the internal counter which starts with 0 and ends with the value in the Horizontal Total register).

This register provides a retrace delay, which may be used to synchronize the retrace and blanking, and other timings based on the end of the horizontal retrace.

Notes: The three most significant digits of the End Horizontal Retrace count are always assumed identical to the three most significant digits of the Start Horizontal Retrace Pulse register.

The adapter always counts the first displayable position as the first scan count. The next intervals include the right overscan, horizontal blanking and retrace, and finally the left overscan.

This register also contains the VGA End Horizontal Blanking overflow bit.

BIOS Default Settings (all values are Hexadecimal):

Mode	0	1	2	3	4	5	6	7	d	e	f	10
	15	15	07	07	14	14	06	60	14	06	e0	ba

More than 64K EGA memory:

Mode	f	10
	60	00

Values for the Enhanced Color Display:

Mode	0	1	2	3
	6d	6d	5b	5b

Bits: 0–4   The five least significant digits of the character count at which the Horizontal Retrace ends.

5–6   00b — No delay
01b — Delay of 1 character
10b — Delay of 2 characters
11b — Delay of 3 characters

7   Start Odd/Even Memory Address (EGA only)
This bit is normally 0. It provides an extra bit for horizontal smooth scrolling on EGAs with

less than 64K memory . The standard sequence (scrolling the display right) is to start this bit set to 0, scroll eight pixels, set this bit to 1, and scroll eight pixels. Then the Start Address is incremented and the scrolling sequence starts again. The equivalent VGA function is performed through the Preset Row Scan register (index 8). NOTE: When less than 64K is installed, this bit is initially 1 (middle of the sequence).

7   End Horizontal Blanking bit 5 (VGA only) The sixth bit of the VGA's End Horizontal Blanking register (see index 3).

Port 3?5h: Vertical Total Register (Index 6)

Description: This register is programmed with the eight least significant bits of the vertical scan line count, plus the period of the vertical retrace. The ninth (high order) bit of the vertical total is programmed in the CRT Controller Overflow register (see index 7). The VGA also uses a tenth bit which appears in the Overflow register.

An internal counter resets after reaching the value programmed into the Vertical Total register. The internal counter is the basis for vertical CRT timings.

BIOS Default Settings (all values are Hexadecimal):

Mode	0	1	2	3	4	5	6	7	d	e	f	10
	04	04	04	04	04	04	04	70	04	04	70	6c

Values for the Enhanced Color Display:

Mode	0	1	2	3
	6c	6c	6c	6c

Bits: 0–7   The eight least significant bits of the full vertical cycle time (programmed as a line count).

Port 3?5h: CRT Controller Overflow Register (Index 7)

Description: This register is programmed with the most
significant (ninth and tenth) bits of the vertical scan
registers.

See the individual registers referenced below for descriptions.

BIOS Default Settings (all values are Hexadecimal):

Mode	0	1	2	3	4	5	6	7	d	e	f	10
	11	11	11	11	11	11	11	1f	11	11	1f	1f

Values for the Enhanced Color Display:

Mode	0	1	2	3
	1f	1f	1f	1f

Bits: 0   Vertical Total.
                      The ninth bit of the Vertical Total register
                      (see index 6).

             1   Vertical Display Enable End.
                      The ninth bit of the Vertical Display Enable
                      End register (see index 12h).

             2   Vertical Retrace Start.
                      The ninth bit of the Vertical Retrace Start
                      register (see index 10h).

             3   Start Vertical Blank.
                      The ninth bit of the Start Vertical Blank
                      register (see index 15h). The VGA's tenth
                      bit is located in the Maximum Scan Line
                      register (see index 9).

             4   Line Compare.
                      The ninth bit of the Line Compare register
                      (see index 18h). The VGA's tenth bit is located
                      in the Maximum Scan Line register
                      (see index 9).

5   Vertical Total (VGA only)
         The tenth bit of the Vertical Total register
         (see index 6).

6   Vertical Display Enable End (VGA only)
         The tenth bit of the Vertical Display Enable
         register (see index 12h).

7   Vertical Retrace Start (VGA only)
         The tenth bit of the Vertical Retrace
         Start register (see index 10h).

Port 3?5h: Preset Row Scan Register (Index 8)

Description: The first displayable scan line is determined by
         the Start Address register (see indexes ch and dh) plus
         an offset determined by this register's setting. This
         register is programmed with the starting row number
         (normally 0).

Notes: This register is used to implement smooth scrolling
         in alphanumeric modes (it should always be set to 0 for
         graphics modes). The Start Address register should
         point to the first character position of the display. In
         graphics modes, the Start Address alone controls verti-
         cal smooth scrolling.

         The value of this register should not exceed the
         current character height. Upon reaching the character
         height (or zero, depending on the scroll direction), the
         display should be scrolled one line and the Preset Row
         Scan register set to zero (or the character height).

         When the Preset Row Scan register is changed, it
         takes effect at the beginning of the following display in-
         terval. If it is changed at any time during the first row's
         display interval, the new setting will activate immediate-
         ly. For this reason, the Preset Row Scan register should
         be set either after the first horizontal retrace or during
         the vertical retrace.

BIOS Default Settings (all values are Hexadecimal):

Mode	0	1	2	3	4	5	6	7	d	e	f	10
	00	00	00	00	00	00	00	00	00	00	00	00

Bits: 0–4   Preset Row Scan (Pel Scrolling)
                         Value of the starting pixel row number after
                         completion of the vertical retrace (usually 0).

               5–6   Byte Panning Control (VGA only)
                         This provides an extra two bits of Horizontal
                         Pel Panning when two or four-bit planes are
                         chained together as a single-bit plane. None
                         of the VGA's BIOS modes chain planes. Modes
                         0fh and 10h on EGAs with less than 64K are
                         the only programmed modes which would
                         require an extra bit, but the equivalent function
                         is located in the EGA's End Horizontal
                         Retrace register (see index 5).

               7   Unused

Port 3?5h: Maximum Scan Line Register (Index 9)

Description: The Maximum Scan Line register is programmed
             with a value of one less than the current character
             height (in pixels).

Notes: This register sets the character height for
             alphanumeric modes only.

BIOS Default Settings (all values are Hexadecimal):

Mode	0	1	2	3	4	5	6	7	d	e	f	10
	07	07	07	07	01	01	01	0d	00	00	00	00

Values for the Enhanced Color Display:

Mode	0	1	2	3
	0d	0d	0d	0d

Bits: 0–4   Maximum Scan Line
                         Value of the alphanumeric character height
                         minus one.

5   Start Vertical Blank (VGA only)
This is the tenth bit of the Start Vertical
Blank register (see index 15h). The ninth
bit is located in the Overflow register
(see index 7).

6   Line Compare Register (VGA only)
This is the tenth bit of the Line Compare
register (see index 18h). The ninth bit is
located in the Overflow register (see index 7).

7   200 to 400-Line Conversion (VGA only)
When this bit is set to 1, each scan line in
200-line modes is displayed twice, giving
an effective resolution of 400 lines (this is
the normal setting). When set to 0, scan
doubling is disabled.

Port 3?5h: **Cursor Start Register (Index ah)**

Description: The Cursor Start register specifies the first row
number of the cursor within the character box. The last
row is set by the Cursor End register (Index bh).

Notes: This register is valid for alphanumeric modes only.

Row numbers start with 0. The value used should
be one less than the starting row number (2 less than
the row). On the EGA, setting the cursor start register
to a higher value than the cursor end register will cause
the cursor to wrap from the bottom of the box to the top,
giving a double line (this is not supported on the VGA
and will cause the cursor to disappear).

The BIOS default settings reflect the values of
the Parameter Table. The Parameter Table values for
the Cursor Start register and Cursor End register are
converted by BIOS to actual value OUTed to the
registers. For example, the actual cursor start value for
mode 0 is 5 for the Color Display and bh for the ECD.

BIOS Default Settings (all values are Hexadecimal):

Mode	0	1	2	3	4	5	6	7	d	e	f	10
	06	06	06	06	00	00	00	0b	00	00	00	00

Bits: 0–4   Cursor Start
                        Value of the first cursor row position minus one.

               5   Cursor Off (VGA only)
                        When set to 1, the VGA cursor is turned off.

               6–7   Unused

Port 3?5h: Cursor End Register (Index bh)

Description: The Cursor End register specifies the last row
                number of the cursor within the character box. The first
                row is set by the Cursor Start register (Index ah).

                The Cursor End register also provides a skew
                control to delay the cursor control signal by 0–3 charac-
                ter clocks.

Notes: This register is valid for alphanumeric modes only.

                Row numbers start with 0. The value used should
                be the starting row number (1 less than the row). On the
                EGA, setting the cursor start register to a higher value
                than the cursor end register will cause the cursor to
                wrap from the bottom of the box to the top, giving a
                double line (this is not supported by the VGA, and will
                cause the cursor to disappear).

                The BIOS default settings reflect the values of
                the Parameter Table. The Parameter table values for
                the Cursor Start register and Cursor End register are
                converted by BIOS to actual value OUTed to the
                registers. For example, the actual cursor end value for
                mode 0 is 7 for the Color Display and dh for the ECD.

BIOS Default Settings (all values are Hexadecimal):

Mode	0	1	2	3	4	5	6	7	d	e	f	10
	07	07	07	07	00	00	00	0c	00	00	00	00

Bits: 0–4   Cursor End
                        Value of the last cursor row position.

5–6   Cursor Skew
00b — No delay
01b — Delay of 1 character
10b — Delay of 2 characters
11b — Delay of 3 characters

7   Unused

Port 3?5h: **Start Address High Register (Index ch)**

Description: The Start Address High register is programmed with the eight most significant bits of the memory address (as seen by the CRTC) of the first displayable character (alpha mode) or pixel (graphics mode). The eight least significant bits are in the Start Address Low register (index dh).

Notes: This is a read/write register.

The Start Address registers are useful for implementing smooth scrolling. Also see the Offset register, index 13h; the Attribute Controller's Horizontal Pel Pan register, port 3c0h, index 13h; and the Preset Row Scan register, index 8.

When the Start Address is changed, it takes effect at the beginning of the following vertical retrace and should therefore be programmed during the active display interval.

When four maps are chained as two, the Start Address register always points to a word boundary. Likewise, if four planes were chained as one (possible on the VGA, although not implemented), the Start Address would always point to a double word address. The EGA provides a method for selecting the proper byte through the End Horizontal Retrace register (index 5). The VGA selects the byte through the Preset Row Scan register (index 8).

Bits: 0–7   Start Address High
The most significant eight bits (of a 16-bit value) of the first display address.

Port 3?5h: Start Address Low Register (Index dh)

Description: The Start Address Low register contains the eight
least significant bits of the memory address (as seen by
the CRTC) of the first displayable character (alpha
mode) or pixel (graphics mode). The eight most significant bits are in the Start Address High register
(index ch).

Notes: This is a read/write register.

The Start Address registers are useful for
implementing smooth scrolling. See the notes for the
Start Address High register (index ch).

Bits: 0–7   Start Address Low
The least significant eight bits
(of a 16-bit value) of the first display address.

Port 3?5h: Cursor Location High Register (Index eh)

Description: The Cursor Location High register contains the
eight most significant bits of the memory address (as
seen by the CRTC) of the cursor location. The eight least
significant bits are in the Cursor Location Low register
(index fh).

Notes: This is a read/write register.

Bits: 0–7   Cursor Location High
The most significant eight bits (of a 16-bit
value) of the cursor location.

Port 3?5h: Cursor Location Low Register (Index fh)

Description: The Cursor Location Low register contains the
eight least significant bits of the memory address (as
seen by the CRTC) of the cursor location. The eight most
significant bits are in the Cursor Location High register
(index eh).

Notes: This is a read/write register.

Bits: 0–7   Cursor Location Low
The least significant eight bits
(of a 16-bit value) of the cursor location.

Port 3?5h: **Vertical Retrace Start Register**
                (Index 10h [write])

Description: This register is programmed with the eight least
significant bits of the count value at which vertical
retrace pulse becomes active. The count is based on the
row scan counter, which starts with 0 and ends with the
value in the Vertical Total register. The Vertical Retrace
Start initializes the beam's move to the top of the screen.

Notes: The adapter always counts the first displayable
scan line as the first scan count. The next intervals include the bottom overscan, vertical blanking and
retrace, and finally the top overscan.

The counting unit is vertical scan lines.

The ninth (most significant) bit of the Vertical
Retrace Start is programmed in the CRT Controller
Overflow register (see index 7). The VGA's tenth bit is
also located in the Overflow register.

The Vertical Retrace Start register is set by writing
index 10h; on the EGA, reading index 10h returns the
Light Pen High register. This register is readable on the
VGA (the VGA does not support a light pen).

BIOS Default Settings (all values are Hexadecimal):

Mode	0	1	2	3	4	5	6	7	d	e	f	10
	e1	e1	e1	e1	e1	e1	e0	5e	e1	e0	5e	5e

Values for the Enhanced Color Display:

Mode	0	1	2	3
	5e	5e	5e	5e

Bits: 0–7   The eight least significant bits of the
Vertical Retrace Start count.

Port 3?5h: Light Pen High Register
(Index 10h [read], EGA only)

Description: When the light pen is triggered, the Light Pen High
register returns the eight most significant bits of the
light pen position (as a display address).

Notes: The Light Pen High Address is obtained by reading
index 10h; writing index 10h sets the Vertical Retrace
Start register.

The VGA does not support a light pen.

Bits: 0–7   The eight most significant bits of the
memory address where the light pen
was last triggered.

Port 3?5h: Vertical Retrace End Register
(Index 11h [write])

Description: This register is programmed with the four least significant bits of the count value at which vertical retrace
pulse becomes inactive. The count is based on the row
scan counter, which starts with 0 and ends with the
value in the Vertical Total register (see index 6). The
Vertical Retrace Start initiates the beam's move to the
top of the screen.

The Vertical Retrace End register also provides for
clearing or enabling the vertical interrupt (IRQ2).

Notes: The counting unit is vertical scan lines.

The adapter always counts the first displayable
scan line as the first scan count. The next intervals include the bottom overscan, vertical blanking and
retrace, and finally the top overscan.

The most significant digits of the Vertical Retrace
End count are always assumed identical to the most significant digits of the Vertical Retrace Start register.

The Vertical Retrace End register is set by writing index 11h; on the EGA, reading index 11h returns the Light Pen Low register. This register is readable on the VGA (the VGA does not support a light pen).

When using the vertical interrupt, the interrupt handler must clear the interrupt (bit 4) and reenable it (bit 5). Note that clearing the interrupt also disables further interrupts until bit 4 is set back to 1 (although a few compatibles require this bit to remain 0 — this is not related to the reversed status bit). Most EGAs will work without reenabling interrupts, however; it is required on the PS/2 (because the PS/2 uses level triggered interrupts rather than edge triggering).

A vertical interrupt may be forced by setting bit 5 low (enabling the interrupt) and then high (disabling it) on edge triggered systems — this can be used to determine the polarity of the Vertical Retrace Status bit, which is reversed on some early EGA compatibles (see Input Status Register Zero of the External registers).

Programs which use IRQ2 should provide a way to handle the final interrupt generated when the interrupt is disabled.

Other hardware may also generate an IRQ2. Input Status Register Zero (see port 3c2h) should be read to determine whether the interrupt was issued by the graphics adapter.

Make sure other bits are left unchanged when modifying the vertical interrupt bits.

BIOS Default Settings (all values are Hexadecimal):

Mode	0	1	2	3	4	5	6	7	d	e	f	10
	24	24	24	24	24	24	23	2e	24	23	2e	2b

Values for the Enhanced Color Display:

Mode	0	1	2	3
	2b	2b	2b	2b

Bits: 0–3 The four least significant bits of the Vertical Retrace End count.

4 Clear Vertical Interrupt
Writing 0 to this bit will clear the most recent vertical interrupt (IRQ2). It will also inactivate the interrupt on the PS/2.

5 Enable Vertical Interrupt
Writing 0 to this bit will enable the vertical interrupt (IRQ2) at the start of each vertical retrace.

6 Select 5 Refresh Cycles (VGA only)
This bit sets the number of RAM refreshes per horizontal scan. It is normally set to 0 for three refreshes per scan. A setting of 1 supports 15.75 kHz monitors which require five refreshes per scan.

7 Protect R0-7 (VGA only)
CRTC register 0–7 may be write protected by setting this bit to 1. Because these registers control timing functions and changing them could cause problems, this bit usually should be set.

Port 3?5h: **Light Pen Low Register
(Index 11h [read], EGA only)**

Description: When the light pen is triggered, the Light Pen Low register returns the eight least significant bits of the light pen position (as a display address).

Notes: The Light Pen Low Address is obtained by reading index 11h; writing index 11h sets the Vertical Retrace End register.

The VGA does not support a light pen.

Bits: 0–7 The eight least significant bits of the memory address where the light pen was last triggered.

Port 3?5h: Vertical Display Enable End Register (Index 12h)

Description: This register is programmed with the eight least
significant bits of the displayable area's vertical scan
line count. The ninth (high order) bit of the vertical total
is programmed in the CRT Controller Overflow register
(see index 7). The VGA has a tenth bit which is also located in the Overflow register.

Note: The value used by the Vertical Display Enable
End register is actually one less than the total number
of scan lines (so that a value of zero designates one line).

BIOS Default Settings (all values are Hexadecimal):

Mode	0	1	2	3	4	5	6	7	d	e	f	10
	c7	c7	c7	c7	c7	c7	c7	5d	c7	c7	5d	5d

Bits: 0–7   The eight least significant bits of the
vertical display area (minus one)

Port 3?5h: Offset Register (Index 13h)

Description: The Offset register allocates the amount of display
memory per row. Memory may be allocated in either
words or double words (see bit 2 of the Clocking Mode
tegister, port 3c5h, index 1). The VGA may also use four
words (bit 4 of the Clocking Mode tegister)

Notes: This is not the displayable screen width; the
Offset register deals only with memory allocation. This
is especially useful for applications which use smooth
horizontal scrolling. The line width may be set larger
than the display width, so that only a portion of the logical screen is displayed. The Start Address may be used
to select the first displayable character position (see indexes ch and dh). Also see the Preset Row Scan register
(index 8) and the Attribute Controller's Horizontal Pel
Pan register (port 3c0h, index 13h).

BIOS Default Settings (all values are Hexadecimal):

Mode	0	1	2	3	4	5	6	7	d	e	f	10
	14	14	28	28	14	14	28	28	14	28	14	14

More than 64K EGA memory:

Mode f 10
      28 28

Bits: 0–7   Offset.
                          Logical screen width (divided by 2, 4, or 8).

Port 3?5h: Underline Location Register (Index 14h)

Description: The Underline Location register sets the position
                of the underline within the character box.

Notes: Positions are numbered beginning with 0 — to set
                the underline to the bottom of a 14-pixel-high character
                cell, the position should be set to 13.

                Underlining is disabled by setting the position
                below the current cell height (this is done in color modes
                to preserve compatibility with the CGA). Underlining
                can be enabled on color monitors.

BIOS Default Settings (all values are Hexadecimal):

Mode	0	1	2	3	4	5	6	7	d	e	f	10
	08	08	08	08	00	00	00	0d	00	00	0d	0f

Values for the Enhanced Color Display:

Mode	0	1	2	3
	0f	0f	0f	0f

Bits: 0–4   Underline Location
                          Position of the underline within the
                          character cell.

             5   Count by 4 (VGA only)
                          Setting this bit to 1 divides the character
                          clock (which updates the memory address
                          counter) by 4; i.e., the memory address is
                          changed once every four clocks.

             6   Double Word Mode (VGA only)
                          Setting this bit to 1 selects double word
                          memory addressing. Bit 6 of the Mode

Control register (index 17h) must be set to
0 for this bit to have effect.

7   Unused

Port 3?5h: **Start Vertical Blanking Register (Index 15h)**

Description: This register is programmed with the eight least
significant bits of the count value at which vertical
blanking begins. The count is based on the row scan
counter, which starts with 0 and ends with the value in
the Vertical Total register (see index 6). The Vertical
Blanking prevents the beam from writing over the display area during the retrace.

Notes: The adapter always counts the first displayable
scan line as the first scan count. The next intervals include the bottom overscan, vertical blanking and
retrace, and finally the top overscan.

The counting unit is vertical scan lines.

The ninth (most significant) bit of the Start
Vertical Blanking register is programmed in the CRT
Controller Overflow Register (see index 7).

The VGA has a tenth bit which is located in the
Maximum Scan Line register (see index 9).

BIOS Default Settings (all values are Hexadecimal):

Mode	0	1	2	3	4	5	6	7	d	e	f	10
	e0	e0	e0	e0	e0	e0	df	5e	e0	df	5e	5f

Values for the Enhanced Color Display:

Mode	0	1	2	3
	5e	5e	5e	5e

Bits: 0–7   The eight least significant bits of the
Start Vertical Blanking count.

Port 3?5h: End Vertical Blanking (Index 16h)

Description: This register is programmed with the five least
significant bits of the count value at which the vertical
blanking interval ends. The count is based on the row
scan counter, which starts with 0 and ends with the
value in the Vertical Total register (see index 6). The
Vertical Retrace Start initializes the beam's move to the
top of the screen.

Notes: The counting unit is vertical scan lines.

The EGA always counts the first displayable scan
line as the first scan count. The next intervals include
the bottom overscan, vertical blanking and retrace, and
finally the top overscan.

For the EGA, the four most significant digits of
the Vertical Retrace End count are always assumed identical to the four most significant digits of the Vertical
Retrace Start register. The VGA assumes only the two
most significant bits are identical — all seven bits of this
register are used.

The EGA parameter table shows some cases where
bits 5–7 are set. The End Vertical Blanking register ig-
nores these bits. For example, the setting of f0h for
mode 0 is the same as 10h.

BIOS Default Settings (all values are Hexadecimal):

Mode	0	1	2	3	4	5	6	7	d	e	f	10
	f0	f0	f0	f0	f0	f0	ef	6e	f0	ef	6e	0a

Values for the Enhanced Color Display:

Mode	0	1	2	3
	0a	0a	0a	0a

Bits: 0–4   EGA only.
The five least significant bits of the
End Vertical Blanking count.

0–7   VGA only.
The eight least significant bits of the
End Vertical Blanking count.

Port 3?5h: Mode Control Register (Index 17h)

Description: This register provides functions for mapping
adapter memory to pixel and attribute data. It is similar
in function to the Sequencer Memory Mode register and
the Graphics Controller Mode and Miscellaneous
registers.

BIOS Default Settings (all values are Hexadecimal):

Mode	0	1	2	3	4	5	6	7	d	e	f	10
	a3	a3	a3	a3	a2	a2	c2	a3	e3	e3	8b	8b

More than 64K EGA memory:

Mode	f	10
	e3	e3

Bits: 0   Compatibility Mode Support
                      Setting this bit to 0 creates two display
                      memory areas, one for the even scan lines
                      and one for the odd scan lines. The start of
                      each area is offset by 8K. This is accomplished
                      by replacing bit 13 of the memory address
                      with the least significant bit (bit 0) of the
                      row counter (which designates even or odd
                      scan lines). This function implements CGA
                      graphics mode address compatibility.

             1   Select Row Scan Counter
                      Setting this bit to 0 replaces bit 14 of the
                      address register with bit 1 of the row counter.
                      This is similar in function to bit 0.

             2   Horizontal Retrace Select
                      When this bit is set to 0, the vertical line
                      counter is incremented during each horizontal
                      retrace (this is the standard usage). When set
                      to 1, the counter is incremented every other
                      horizontal retrace; i.e., the horizontal retrace
                      is divided by two. Using divide by two doubles
                      the maximum vertical resolution to 1024 lines
                      on the EGA (2048 lines on the VGA) by giving
                      two vertical lines for each vertical line count.

3   Count by Two
Setting this bit to 0 increments the memory
address on every character clock, selecting a
byte refresh address. A setting of 1 increments
the address every other character clock
(the character clock is divided by two),
selecting a word refresh address.

4   Output Control (EGA only)
During normal operation, this bit is always
set to 0. Setting this bit to 1 places all outputs
in a high impedance state.

5   Address Wrap
This bit may be used in conjunction with the
word or byte mode (see bit 6 of this register).
In byte mode, this bit has no effect. When in
word mode, setting this bit to 1 places
memory address bit 15 on address bit 0, and
a setting of 0 places memory address bit 13
on address bit 0. Bit 13 is used to support bit
plane chaining in high resolution graphics
modes when less than 64K is installed on
the EGA.

6   Word Mode or Byte Mode
Byte mode is selected by setting this bit to 1,
and word mode by setting it to 0. Word mode
supports alternation of data between two bit
planes, e.g., character and attribute data or
for chaining bit planes (see bit 5 of this
register). Word mode rotates the address
bits, moving each bit to a higher position
and bringing either bit 13 or 15 into bit 0.
The VGA also supports a double word mode
(see the Underline Location register, index
14, bit 6) in which case the address bits
are rotated two positions. In double word mode,
bits 0 and 1 are replaced by bits 12 and 13,
respectively.

7   Hardware Reset
Setting this bit to 1 enables the vertical and
horizontal retraces (normal operation). A
setting of 0 clears the retraces.

Port 3?5h: **Line Compare Register (Index 18h)**

Description: This register is programmed with the eight least significant bits of the count value at which the line counter is cleared. The count is based on the row scan counter, which starts with 0 and ends with the value in the Vertical Total register (see index 6). The Line Compare prevents a portion of the screen from scrolling, and can be used to implement a second window.

The Start Address registers specify the memory displayed for the first portion of the screen. Upon reaching the line count, the display switches to memory address 0. The second window always begins at address 0.

Notes: The adapter always counts the first displayable scan line as the first scan count. The next intervals include the bottom overscan, vertical blanking and retrace, and finally the top overscan.

The counting unit is vertical scan lines.

The ninth (most significant) bit of the Line Compare register is programmed in the CRT Controller Overflow register (see index 7). The VGA has a tenth bit located in the Maximum Scan Line register (see index 9).

An even line compare value should be used for 200 line modes.

BIOS Default Settings (all values are Hexadecimal):

Mode	0	1	2	3	4	5	6	7	d	e	f	10
	ff	ff	ff	ff	ff	ff	ff	ff	ff	ff	ff	ff

Bits: 0–7   The eight least significant bits of the Line Compare value.

9

The Graphics Controller Registers

The Graphics Controller registers manipulate data as it is moved between the CPU and EGA memory. They also pass data from the bit plane memory to the Attribute Controller as serial bit streams when graphics mode is enabled. Several of the Graphics Controller registers control the CGA emulation modes. A better understanding of the adapter's internal operations may help clarify the functions of these registers.

Each bit plane of memory has one eight-bit latch register. In graphics mode, data is not written to (or read from) memory; rather, an onboard ALU (Arithmetic Logic Unit) combines data from the CPU with the latch registers. There are four of these latch registers (one from each plane) which hold the contents of the most recently read adapter memory address. Combined data is then written to memory. Since the latch registers hold a full byte of data (and frequently only a single bit is modified), it is important that they contain the current data to prevent changing unmodified data. The latch registers should be loaded with the current memory contents before they are modified by MOVing data from graphics memory to a CPU register, e.g., MOV AL,ES:[BX] where ES:[BX] points to EGA memory. Usually, the actual value read by the CPU is ignored, although the meaning of this data may be controlled through the read mode.

The Graphics Control registers control the technique by which the CPU and latch register data is combined. For example, data can be ANDed, ORed, or XORed; bit planes can be "permanently" turned off or on; and bit positions can be masked as unaffected. Note that one function you might expect to appear here, the bit map mask, is a function of the Sequencer register.

Port 3cah: Graphics 2 Position Register (EGA only)

Description: The EGA contains two Graphics Controller chips,
each of which controls two planes (for a total of four bit
planes). These two chips are referred to as Graphics 1
and Graphics 2. The Graphics 2 Position register selects
which two bits of the CPU data bus affect the Graphics 2
chip; i.e., which color planes are controlled by Graphics
1 (note that there is an extra bit allotted for this function — only one bit is necessary for four bit planes).

Notes: This chip should always be programmed for
position 1.

This is the read address for the VGA feature
Control register (see port 3?ah of the External registers).

BIOS Default Settings (all values are Hexadecimal):

Mode	0	1	2	3	4	5	6	7	d	e	f	10
	01	01	01	01	01	01	01	01	01	01	01	01

Bits: 0–1   Position number

2–7   Unused

Port 3cch: Graphics 1 Position Register (EGA only)

Description: The EGA contains two Graphics Controller chips,
each of which controls two planes (for a total of four bit
planes). These two chips are referred to as Graphics 1
and Graphics 2. The Graphics 1 Position register selects
which two bits of the CPU data bus affect the Graphics 1
chip, i.e., which color planes are controlled by Graphics
1 (note that there is an extra bit allotted for this function — only one bit is necessary for four bit planes).

Notes: This chip should always be programmed for
position 0.

This is the read address for the VGA
Miscellaneous Output register (see port 3c2h of the External registers).

BIOS Default Settings (all values are Hexadecimal):

Mode	0	1	2	3	4	5	6	7	d	e	f	10
	00	00	00	00	00	00	00	00	00	00	00	00

Bits: 0–1   Position number

            2–7   Unused

Port 3ceh: Graphics 1 and 2 Address Register

Description: The Graphics 1 and 2 Address register selects
which register will appear at port 3cfh. The index number of the desired register is OUTed to port 3ceh.

Index   Register

            0   Set/Reset
            1   Enable Set/Reset
            2   Color Compare
            3   Data Rotate
            4   Read Map Select
            5   Mode Register
            6   Miscellaneous
            7   Color Don't Care
            8   Bit Mask

Port 3cfh: Set/Reset Register (Index 0)

Description: The Set/Reset register may be used to select bit
planes as "permanently" set or cleared. Placing a bit
plane in set mode will always write 1 to the masked
bit(s) during a memory write. Placing a bit plane in
reset mode will always write 0 to the masked bits.

This register can be used to write an absolute
color to memory (unaffected by logical functions), limit
the number of colors available by always keeping a particular bit plane (or planes) turned on or off, or clear
planes disabled by the Bit Mask register.

Notes: This register affects only write mode 0 (see the
description of the Mode register, index 5).

You must also enable the Set/Reset through the Enable Set/Reset register (index 1). Otherwise, all bit planes would always be set or reset during a write in mode 0. The VGA provides write mode 3 which uses the Set/Reset register directly (it is not necessary to use the Enable Set/Reset register, see the Mode register).

BIOS Default Settings (all values are Hexadecimal):

Mode	0	1	2	3	4	5	6	7	d	e	f	10
	00	00	00	00	00	00	00	00	00	00	00	00

Bits:	0	Set/Reset bit plane 0
	1	Set/Reset bit plane 1
	2	Set/Reset bit plane 2
	3	Set/Reset bit plane 3

Port 3cfh: Enable Set/Reset Register (Index 1)

Description: The Set/Reset register may be used to "permanently" enable or disable a memory plane selected via the Set/Reset register.

Notes: This register affects only write mode 0 (see the description of the mode register below).

You must specify the set or reset function through the Set/Reset register before enabling it with this register.

BIOS Default Settings (all values are Hexadecimal):

Mode	0	1	2	3	4	5	6	7	d	e	f	10
	00	00	00	00	00	00	00	00	00	00	00	00

Bit:	0	Enable Set/Reset for bit plane 0
	1	Enable Set/Reset for bit plane 1
	2	Enable Set/Reset for bit plane 2
	3	Enable Set/Reset for bit plane 3

Programming Example:

These two short programs were written to work with DOS (BASICA) 3.2. Assemble the assembly program (name it SET_RST) and the run the BASIC program.

The SET_RST program sets the registers to always write 0 to bit plane 0. This is quite noticeable in the printed numerals — there are only eight colors. However, the bars appear in 16 colors, and the circle is white despite the lack of white amongst the numerals. So what is happening here?

As noted above, the Set/Reset registers only affect write mode 0. The character printing routines are using this mode, and are thus limited to eight colors. However, the line and circle routines must be using write mode 2 and thus remain unaffected. Write Mode 0 usually works best for writing eight-bit patterns (such as a character mask), while write mode 2 usually works best for plotting routines — this is reflected in BASIC's internal use of these modes.

```
10      CLS: KEY OFF
20      SCREEN 9
30      SHELL "set_rst"
40      FOR I%= 0 TO 15
50         FOR J%=0 TO 20
60               LINE (0+I%*20+J%,40)-(40+I%*20+J%,200),I%
70         NEXT J%
80      NEXT I%
90      CIRCLE (320,170),150
100     LOCATE 20,1
110     FOR I%=1 TO 15
120         COLOR I%: PRINT I%;
130     NEXT I%
```

```
cseg        segment 'public'
            assume  CS:cseg

main        proc    far

start:

            push    DS
            sub     AX,AX
            push    AX
```

```
        mov     DX,3ceh     ;Graphics 1 and 2 address
        mov     AL,0        ;Set/Reset register index
        out     DX,AL
        inc     DX          ;Set/Reset register address
        mov     AL,0000b    ;Choose Reset for all planes
        out     DX,AL

        dec     DX          ;Graphics 1 and 2 address
        mov     AL,1        ;Enable Set/Reset register index
        out     DX,AL
        inc     DX          ;Enable Set/Reset register address
        mov     AL,0001b    ;Only enable plane 0
                            ; the reset will only affect plane 1

        out     DX,AL

        ret

main    endp

cseg    ends

end     start
```

Port 3cfh: Color Compare Register (Index 2)

Description: The Color Compare register, as its name suggests,
             compares the register color with the contents of the
             adapter's memory. The color value is first written to the
             Color Compare register, and then memory is read. The
             bits read will be 1 where the color is the same as the
             Color Compare register, and 0 where they differ (thus
             eight pixels can be compared in per CPU read). This
             register works only in read mode 1 (see the Mode
             register, index 5). The actual value of any bit plane may
             be ignored (assumed matching) by using the Color Don't
             Care register (see index 7).

BIOS Default Settings (all values are Hexadecimal):

Mode	0	1	2	3	4	5	6	7	d	e	f	10
	00	00	00	00	00	00	00	00	00	00	00	00

Bits: 0–3   Color number to be compared

            4–8   Not used

Port 3cfh: Data Rotate Register (Index 3)

Description: The Data Rotate register performs two functions. As implied by the name, the data written by the CPU can be set to rotate right n places (this is usually set to 0).

Additionally, this register provides a logical function which specifies how the data is combined with the current contents of the latch registers. Data can be overwritten, ANDed, ORed, or XORed.

Notes: When both a rotate and logical function are applied, the rotate will occur first.

This register will not affect write mode 1. It only affects data written from the CPU to the adapter.

The rotate count affects only write mode 0.

BIOS Default Settings (all values are Hexadecimal):

Mode	0	1	2	3	4	5	6	7	d	e	f	10
	00	00	00	00	00	00	00	00	00	00	00	00

Bits: 0–2   Rotate count. Rotate data n positions to the right where $0 < = n < = 7$.

3–4   Function select
   00b   Write data without modification
   01b   AND data with latch contents
   10b   OR data with latch contents
   11b   XOR data with latch contents

5–7   Not used

Assembly Language Example:

This program writes italic characters to the screen (the program is halted by typing Ctrl-Z). Note that italics are emulated very well by rotating the top five pixels one position to the right, leaving the middle three pixels in their original positions, and rotating the bottom six pixels seven to the right (which has the same effect as one to the left). The far right pixel has been masked as unwritable to prevent dots from rotating off the left side onto the right (the default character always keeps the right pixel blank, so the left side does not need masking).

Since several lines of data are rotated the same amount when writing italics, using the adapter hardware may be more efficient than having the CPU shift the data, since the count does not need to be reset for each new line, and the full shift count occurs in one cycle. In fact, the EGA and VGA seem to be designed for efficient character writing — eight bits can be written to the display and each character is eight bits wide, and the default write mode handles eight pixel writes much better than single pixel plotting. The rotate and mask register could be used for proportional spacing to gain an even greater increase in efficiency. The rotate and mask would allow each row of a character to align on any pixel position, and the mask could be used to split the character between two character cells when necessary. Note that the current contents of any addressed cells should be preserved to prevent overwriting another character sharing the same cell(s).

```
data        segment 'public'

            ega_seg dw      0a000h
            row     dw      10
            col     dw      5
            cols    dw      80
            v_dots  db      14
            ital    db      'Italics'

data        ends

code        segment 'public'

            assume  CS:code

main        proc    far

start:

            push    DS
            sub     AX,AX
            push    AX
            mov     AX,data
            mov     DS,AX
            assume  DS:data

            mov     AX,10h      ;mode 10h
            int     10h
```

```
              mov     AX,1130h   ;put character set location in ES:BP
              mov     BH,1       ;get the current character set
              int     10h
              assume  ES:nothing

agn:          mov     AH,6       ;DOS direct console I/O
              mov     DL,0ffh
              int     21h        ;DOS function call
              jz      agn        ;if no character, try again

              mov     AH,0
              cmp     AL,26      ;was it Ctrl-Z ?
              je      done       ;yes, leave the routine

              mul     v_dots     ;multiply by vertical dots per
                                 ;character
              add     AX,BP      ;AX = offset of character
                                 ;definition
              call    it_out
              add     col,1
              cmp     col,80
              jb      same_row
              mov     col,0
              add     row,1

same_row:
              jmp     agn

done:         ret

main          endp

it_out        proc    near

              mov     CX,0       ;clear the CX register
              mov     SI,AX      ;source is offset of character
              mov     DI,cols    ;store number of columns in
                                 ;DI for later use

              mov     AX,row     ;get the cursor row
              mul     v_dots     ;multiply by dots/pixel to get
                                 ;pixel row
              mul     DI         ;multiply by columns
              add     AX,col     ;and finally add the column to
                                 ;get the offset
              mov     BX,AX      ;mov offset to BX
```

```
            push    DS

            mov     AX,0a000h   ;segment containing mode 10
                                  memory
            mov     DS,AX
            assume  DS:nothing

            mov     DX,3ceh     ;Graphics 1 and 2 Address
            mov     AL,8        ;Index of Bit Mask
            out     DX,AL
            inc     DX          ;Bit Mask register
            mov     AL,11111110b    ;Don't allow writes to
                                      far right bit
            out     DX,AL

            dec     DX          ;Graphics 1 and 2 Address
            mov     AL,3        ;Index of Data Rotate register
            out     DX,AL
            inc     DX          ;Data Rotate register
            mov     AL,10001b   ;Rotate 1 position and OR
                                  with current contents
            out     DX,AL

            mov     CL,5        ;five repetitions
top:        mov     AL,[BX]
                                ;latch the data
            mov     AL,ES:[SI]  ;get the character data
            mov     [BX],AL     ;write data screen
            add     BX,DI
            inc     SI
            loop    top

            mov     AL,10000b   ;No rotate and OR with
                                  current contents
            out     DX,AL

            mov     CL,3        ;three repetitions

mid:        mov     AL,[BX]     ;latch the data
            mov     AL,ES:[SI]
                                ;get the character data
            mov     [BX],AL
                                ;write data screen
            add     BX,DI
            inc     SI
            loop    mid
```

```
            mov     AL,10111b  ;rotate 7 positions and OR
                               with current contents
            out     DX,AL

            mov     CL,6       ;six repetitions

bot:        mov     AL,[BX]
                               ;latch the data
            mov     AL,ES:[SI] ;get the character data
            mov     [BX],AL    ;write data screen
            add     BX,DI
            inc     SI
            loop    bot

            pop     DS

            ret

it_out      endp

code        ends

end         start
```

Port 3cfh: Read Map Select Register (Index 4)

Description: A byte of any single bit plane may be read from display
memory by the CPU by writing the desired plane's number (0, 1, 2, or 3) to the Read Map Select register.

Notes: This register only functions in read mode 0 (see bit
4 of the next entry — the mode register). Read mode 0 is
the BIOS default, so setting the read mode usually is not
necessary.

BIOS Default Settings (all values are Hexadecimal):

Mode	0	1	2	3	4	5	6	7	d	e	f	10
	00	00	00	00	00	00	00	00	00	00	00	00

Bits: 0–1   Number of bit plane to be read

           2–7   Not used

Port 3cfh: Mode Register (Index 5)

Description: This register must first be selected by writing the value 4 to the Graphics 1 and 2 Address register (port 3ceh).

The adapter provides three methods for writing data and two methods for reading data. By switching to a mode that best reflects your procedure's requirements, the speed of setting or reading pixels can be significantly improved.

The Mode register (in conjunction with the Miscellaneous register, index 6) provides CPU addressing functions. Similar functions are available through the Sequencer Memory Mode register and the CRTC Mode Control register.

Notes: BIOS uses write mode 0 and read mode 0 as the defaults.

When writing data directly to adapter memory, it is important to first load the latch registers with the current memory contents. This is done by MOVing data from adapter memory to the CPU (e.g. mov AL,ES:[BX]).

BIOS Default Settings (all values are Hexadecimal):

Mode	0	1	2	3	4	5	6	7	d	e	f	10
	10	10	10	10	30	30	00	10	00	00	10	10

More than 64K EGA memory:

Mode	f	1
	00	00

Bits: 0–1   Write Mode
0 — The Map Mask register is used to enable or disable bit planes for writing, and the Bit Mask register is used to enable or disable pixels within the byte. Data moved into adapter memory is written to each enabled plane (except those enabled for Set/Reset — see the Set/Reset register, index 0) and pixel. Thus, mov ES:[BX],9 would write the pattern 10000001b to the

enabled bit planes (turing on the first and eighth pixel and turning off the second through seventh pixels).

1 The contents of the latch registers are written to memory. Each bit plane has an eight-bit latch register, which is loaded when the CPU reads adapter memory. Normally, the data is combined from the CPU and latch registers and then written to adapter memory, but this mode writes from the latch registers only. This is useful for loading the latches from one memory location and writing them to another; e.g., commonly used images may be stored in an unused portion of memory, and transferred by simple MOVes without setting registers to change colors (although nothing in the overwritten areas will be preserved).

2 The Bit Mask register is used to enable or disable the specific pixels within the one-byte address written by the CPU. The CPU data specifies which color is written. Thus, mov ES:[BX],4 would write color 4 to the enabled pixels. This is also the write mode used by IBM BASICA 3.2 (see the programming example for the Enable Set/Reset register, index 1).

3 VGA only. The Set/Reset value is ANDed with the Bit Mask register (see index 8) and written to the designated adapter address. The Enable Set/Reset register need not be set for this write mode.

2 Test Condition (EGA only)
Setting this bit to 1 places the controller outputs in high impedance state. Unless you are doing diagnostics, this bit should always be set to 0.

3 Read Mode

0 Each bit set when the CPU reads memory designates a bit set in the bit plane chosen by the read map select register.

1   Each bit set when the CPU reads memory designates bits which are the same color as the color in the Color Compare register (see index 2). The result of the read is also affected by the Color Don't Care register (see index 7).

4   Odd/Even
When this bit is set to 1, CPU data at odd addresses are mapped to the odd bit planes (and even addresses to even bit planes). This only affects the Graphics Controllers. Typically, the Sequencer is set to use the same scheme through bit 2 of the Memory Mode register (see the Sequencer Registers). This is useful for alphanumeric modes (attribute data in one plane, character data in the other), emulation of CGA graphics modes, or addressing two bit planes as one when less than 64K is available.

5   Shift Register
When this bit is set, even-numbered bits are written from graphics memory to the even bit planes of the Attribute Controller. Likewise, odd-numbered bits are written to the odd planes. Thus, two sequential memory bits, forming one color, are placed in two separate serial bit streams by the serializer. This allows emulation of CGA four color graphics (two sequential bits form one color by mapping to two separate bit planes).

6   256 Color Mode (VGA only)
This is similar to the shift register (bit 5). As data is serialized, each byte is converted to a 2 x 4 bit array for the Attribute Controller. Since each pixel is represented by two sequential bits of four parallel streams (instead of one sequential bit with four in parallel), several of the Attribute Controller functions do not work in 256 color mode.

7   Not used

Port 3cfh: Miscellaneous Register (Index 6)

Description: This register (in conjunction with the Mode register, index 5) modifies several addressing functions of the Graphics Controller. Similar functions are provided by the Sequencer Memory Mode register and the CRTC Mode Control register.

Bits: 0   Graphics Mode
                   This bit is set to 1 for graphics mode and 0 for alphanumeric mode. Graphics mode disables the bit plane character generator and enables pixel addressing.

           1   Chain Odd Maps to Even Maps
                   This is typically used with bit 4 of the Mode register (see index 5). Odd CPU addresses are written to odd bit planes, and even addresses to even planes. However, the CPU address is first modified by replacing the least significant address bit with bit 13 or 15 (depending on the amount of memory installed on the adapter). The effect is to place low addresses in planes 0 and 2 (which alternate based on the actual CPU's least significant bit if Odd/Even mode is in effect) and high addresses in planes 1 and 3. Thus, the odd bit planes follow the even planes in the CPU's address space, doubling the effective address space on adapters with less than 64K memory.

           2–3   Memory Map
                   These bits set the location and size of the memory map (for direct memory access by the CPU). No other display adapter may be installed when the value is 00b since the memory addresses of the two adapters would conflict.

                   00b A000h / 128K
                   01b A000h / 64K
                   10b B000h / 32K
                   11b B800h / 32K

           4–7   Not used

Port 3cfh: Color Don't Care Register (Index 7)

Description: This register allows the CPU to ignore the specified bit plane(s) when reading EGA memory via the Color Compare register and read mode 1 (see the Color Compare register, index 2, and the Mode register, index 5).

This register should be set to fh to match only the color in the Color Compare register (a setting of 0 will match any color).

Bits: 0   When set to 0, the contents of bit plane 0 are assumed to match the Color Compare setting for bit plane 0.

             1   When set to 0, the contents of bit plane 1 are assumed to match the Color Compare setting for bit plane 1.

             2   When set to 0, the contents of bit plane 2 are assumed to match the Color Compare setting for bit plane 2.

             3   When set to 0, the contents of bit plane 3 are assumed to match the Color Compare setting for bit plane 3.

             4–7   Not used

Port 3cfh: Bit Mask Register (Index 8)

Description: The Bit Mask register enables or disables modification of any or all bits within the one-byte address written by the CPU. For single pixel plotting, only a single bit should be enabled. Enabling multiple bits is useful for writing characters (in graphics mode) and horizontal lines.

Notes: The current data must be latched in order to be preserved. This is done by performing a CPU read before every write.

This register does not affect write mode 1.

Bits: 0–7 Each bit set to 1 allows that bit to be changed by the CPU. Each bit set to 0 prevents that bit from changing. For example, 0 prevents any memory bits from changing, and ffh allows all eight bits to change.

10

The Attribute Controller Registers

The Attribute Controller registers control the color assignments for the color numbers, overscan, and background. Although undocumented, the registers will respond at port 3c1h. This feature allows a single out instruction to select and program the register, just as with the other output registers. In graphics modes, memory data is usually passed to the Attribute Controller in the form of four serial bit streams (one stream from each bit plane). On every dot clock, the video serializers pass a bit from each serial stream. The Attribute Controller uses the four bit value to look up the color to be displayed (or, in the case of the VGA, four additional static bits are added, and the resulting eight-bit value is passed to the DAC). The Sequencer loads the serializer every character clock (eight or nine bits), unless bit planes are being chained. Figure 10-1 illustrates this sequence.

The attribute registers should only be changed during a vertical retrace.

Port 3c0h: Attribute Address Register

Description: The Attribute Address register selects which register will appear at port 3c0h. The index number of the desired register is written to port 3c0h. Because port 3c0h is shared by both the Address and indexed registers, the Address register should always be initialized. Performing an IN from Input Status Register One at port 3bah (monochrome) or 3dah (color) will always set the register to the Address function.

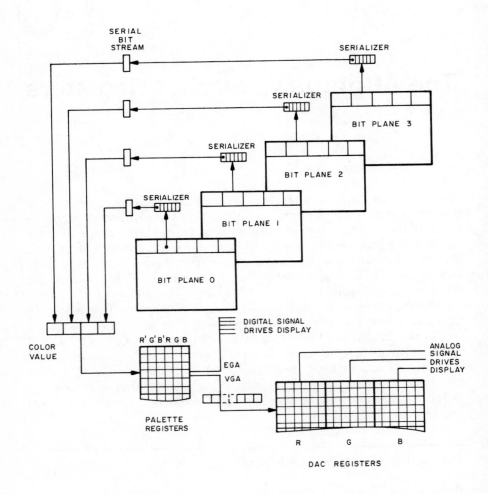

Figure 10-1 Data flow from memory to the CRT

Index   Register

                 0-fh   Palette registers
                 10   Mode Control
                 11   Overscan Color
                 12   Color Plane Enable
                 13   Horizontal Pel Panning
                 14   Color Select (VGA only)

Notes: The Attribute registers should only be set during
                 a vertical retrace.

                 Bit 5 must be set to 0 (disabling EGA access)
                 before the palette registers are modified, and reset to 1
                 after the settings are completed.

                 On the VGA, the attribute registers may be read
                 from 3c1h.

Bits: 0–4   Attribute Address
                           This is the index number of the register
                           to be addressed.

                 5   Palette Address
                           Setting this bit to 1 enables the EGA's
                           internal registers to access the palette data;
                           0 disables access.

                 6–7   Not used

Port 3c0h: Palette Registers (Index 0-fh)

Description: On the EGA, these 16 registers control the actual
             color displayed by each of the color numbers (bit plane
             combinations). Indices 0–15 control colors 0–15, respec-
             tively. The default color scheme is organized such that
             adding two color numbers gives the color formed by that
             mix; e.g., color 1 (blue) + color 2 (green) gives color 3
             (cyan = the combination of blue and green). The primary
             colors blue, green, and red appear in the normalized bi-
             nary sequence 1, 2, 4. Colors 8–15 are the intensified ver-
             sions of colors 0–7. The default colors for the ECD are:

Color	R'G'B'R G B	Value
Bit	5 4 3 2 1 0	
Black	0 0 0 0 0 0	0
Blue	0 0 0 0 0 1	1
Green	0 0 0 0 1 0	2
Cyan	0 0 0 0 1 1	3
Red	0 0 0 1 0 0	4
Magenta	0 0 0 1 0 1	5
Brown	0 1 0 1 0 0	14h
White	0 0 0 1 1 1	7
Dk. Gray	1 1 1 0 0 0	38h
L. Blue	1 1 1 0 0 1	39h
L. Green	1 1 1 0 1 0	3ah
L. Cyan	1 1 1 0 1 1	3bh
L. Red	1 1 1 1 0 0	3ch
L. Magenta	1 1 1 1 0 1	3dh
Yellow	1 1 1 1 1 0	3eh
I. White	1 1 1 1 1 1	3fh

Notes: The primary (RGB) and secondary (R'G'B') refer
only to digital-type monitors. The VGA's analog
monitors use a digital to analog converter (DAC) to convert the palette settings to the appropriate color. In fact,
the DAC acts as the palette from which the actual colors
are selected — these palette registers act only as an
index for the DAC's internal color table (an offset may
be specified through the Color Select register, index 14h).

These registers do not affect VGA mode 13h. The
eight-bit color values of this mode are sent directly to
the DAC.

The palette registers should only be set during a
vertical retrace.

On the VGA, the attribute registers may be read
from 3c1h.

BIOS Default Settings (all values are Hexadecimal):

Mode Index	0-3	4-5	6	7	d-e	64K mem		f	10	ECD 0-3
						f	10			
0	00	00	00	00	00	00	00	00	00	00
1	01	13	17	08	01	08	01	08	01	01
2	02	15	17	08	02	00	00	00	02	02
3	03	17	17	08	03	00	00	00	03	03
4	04	02	17	08	04	18	04	18	04	04
5	05	04	17	08	05	18	07	18	05	05
6	06	06	17	08	06	00	00	00	14	14
7	07	07	17	08	07	00	00	00	07	07
8	10	10	17	10	10	00	00	00	38	38
9	11	11	17	18	11	08	01	08	39	39
a	12	12	17	18	12	00	00	00	3a	3a
b	13	13	17	18	13	00	00	00	3b	3b
c	14	14	17	18	14	00	04	00	3c	3c
d	15	15	17	18	15	18	07	18	3d	3d
e	16	16	17	18	16	00	00	00	3e	3e
f	17	17	17	18	17	00	00	00	3f	3f

Bits: EGA:

0   Primary Blue (Color Display/ECD)

1   Primary Green (Color Display/ECD)

2   Primary Red (Color Display/ECD)

3   Secondary Blue (ECD) or Primary Video (Mono)

4   Secondary Green (ECD) or Intensity (Color Displays which support intensity)

5   Secondary Red (ECD)

6–7   Not used

VGA: 0–5   Palette
Selects a color from one of the DAC registers (the DAC uses 256 18-bit color registers to provide a selection from 262,144 colors). The value may be modified by the Mode Control register (index 10h) and Color Select register (index 14h)

6–7   Not used

Port 3c0h: Mode Control Register (Index 10h)

Description: This register selects mode characteristics for the Attribute Controller.

Notes: Bit 3 can be used to enable blinking on color graphics systems in graphics modes. The blink produced is an alternation between two palette colors rather than an on/off blink. For example, color 15 alternates between colors 15 and 8.

              On the VGA, the attribute registers may be read from 3c1h.

BIOS Default Settings (all values are Hexadecimal):

Mode	0	1	2	3	4	5	6	7	d	e	f	10
	08	08	08	08	01	01	01	0e	01	01	0b	01

Bits: 0   Graphics/Alphanumeric Mode
                      Setting this bit to 1 designates graphics mode (0 is alphanumeric mode)

             1   Monochrome Display/Color Display
                      Setting this bit to 1 designates monochrome display attributes. 0 designates color display attributes.

             2   Enable Line Graphics Character Codes
                      This bit is used with mode 7 to support 9-bit-wide line graphics characters on the monochrome display. When set to 1 the ninth dot of characters c0h-dfh will be the same as the eighth dot, and thus line graphics characters will form unbroken horizontal lines. If set to 0, the ninth dot will always be the same color as the background.

             3   Enable Blink/Set Background Intensity
                      This bit toggles between high intensity background or blinking characters based on bit 7 of the attribute byte in alphanumeric modes (this supports the CGA function of selecting either 16 background colors, or eight background colors with and without blinking). Setting this bit to 1 selects attribute

bit 7 as a blink bit (it also allows blinking in graphics modes). Setting this bit to 0 selects attribute bit 7 as a high intensity background bit (and prevents blinking in graphics modes).

4   Not used

5   PEL Panning Compatibility (VGA Only)
Setting this bit to 1 sets the PEL Panning register (see index 13h) to 0 after the line compare and until the vertical retrace (upon reaching the vertical retrace, the PEL Pan register is reloaded with the programmed value). This allows panning only the upper window when split screen mode is enabled. Setting this bit to 0 causes the PEL Panning register to ignore the line compare.

6   PEL Width (VGA Only)
A setting of 1 makes each pixel eight bits wide (used for mode 13h) for a total of 256 colors. All other modes should set this bit to 0.

7   P5, P4 Select (VGA Only)
This bit controls bits 4 and 5 of the palette registers when used to select color values from the DAC table. When set to 1, bits 4 and 5 of the Palette registers (indices 0-fh) are replaced by bits 0 and 1 of the Color Select register (index 14h). When set to 0, the values sent from the Palette registers to the DAC remain unmodified.

Port 3c0h: Overscan Color Register (Index 11h)

Description: This register selects the intensity of each electron gun between the retrace and blanking intervals, resulting in a colored border.

Notes: The BIOS default is 0 (black) for all modes.

The high resolution modes of the EGA do not work properly with colors other than black. The timing constraints of the EGA/ECD combination require the overscan to begin before the electron beam has finished moving to the left side of the screen. Additionally, the borders produced in the highest resolution modes do not extend much past the active display area. Likewise, the use of borders on the VGA is limited.

On the VGA, the attribute registers may be read from 3c1h.

Bits:	0	Primary Blue (Color Display/ECD)
	1	Primary Green (Color Display/ECD)
	2	Primary Red (Color Display/ECD)
	3	Secondary Blue (ECD) or Primary Video (Mono)
	4	Secondary Green (ECD) or Intensity (Color Displays which support intensity)
	5	Secondary Red (ECD)
	6–7	Not used
VGA:	0–7	Palette Selects a color from one of the DAC registers (the DAC uses 256 18-bit color registers to provide a selection from 262,144 colors).

Port 3c0h: Color Plane Enable Register (Index 12h)

Description: This register selects the bit planes used. It may be used to limit bit plane access for compatibility modes and EGAs with less than 64K installed memory.

Notes: On the VGA, the attribute registers may be read from 3c1h.

BIOS Default Settings (all values are Hexadecimal):

Mode	0	1	2	3	4	5	6	7	d	e	f	10
	0f	0f	0f	0f	03	03	01	0f	0f	0f	05	05

More than 64K EGA memory:

Mode	f	10
	05	0f

111111111111111111

CLEAN:

Bits:

0 — When set to 1, bit plane 0 is enabled.

1 — When set to 1, bit plane 1 is enabled.

2 — When set to 1, bit plane 2 is enabled.

3 — When set to 1, bit plane 3 is enabled.

4–5 — Video Status MUX
These bits are used for diagnostics. Two attribute bits (selected via these two bits) appear on bits 4 and 5 of Input Status Register One (see the External registers port 3?ah) according to the following table:

Value	EGA	VGA
00b	Red/Blue	Bit 2/Bit 0
01b	Blue'/Green	Bit 5/Bit 4
10b	Red'/Green'	Bit 3/Bit 1
11b	N/A	Bit 7/Bit 6

6–7 — Not used

Port 3c0h: Horizontal PEL Panning Register (Index 13h)

Description: The Horizontal PEL Panning register shifts the image left by the designated number of pixels. This function is available in either alpha or graphics modes.

Notes: This register should only be set during a vertical retrace.

The Offset register (see the CRTC registers, port 3?5h, index 13h) can be used to select a logical screen width larger than the physical display width. The Start Address register (see port 3?5h, indexes ch and dh) may be used to shift the image right or left one character. This, in conjunction with bit shifts to the left, may be used to implement a PEL Pan to the right or left. When bit planes are chained, the shift registers load 16 or 32 pixels instead of the usual eight, and the Start Address can only point to every second or fourth character. In these cases, the End Horizontal register (see port 3?5h, index 5) assists the EGA, and the Preset Row Scan register (see port 3?5h, index 8) assists the VGA.

Graphics and color modes are limited to a maximum shift of eight pixels. The monochrome alpha mode (7) may be shifted a maximum of nine pixels.

On the VGA, the attribute registers may be read from 3c1h.

Note that mode 7 and VGA modes 0–3 must start with a value of 8 (100b) rather than 0.

BIOS Default Settings (all values are Hexadecimal):

Mode	0	1	2	3	4	5	6	7	d	e	f	10
	00	00	00	00	00	00	00	08	00	00	00	00

Bits: 0–3   Horizontal PEL Panning
                        This value represents the number of bits to
                        shift left (moving the display to the right)
                        according to the following table:

	Modes		
Value	7, 0-3 VGA	13h VGA	All Others
000b	1	0	0
001b	2	N/A	1
010b	3	1	2
011b	4	N/A	3
100b	5	2	4
101b	6	N/A	5
110b	7	3	6
111b	8	N/A	7
100b	0	N/A	N/A

Port 3c0h: VGA Only. Color Select Register (Index 14h)

Description: This register adds additional flexibility in selecting VGA colors. It adds two bits to the palette registers to provide a full eight bit palette selection (256 colors). The two most significant bits of the palette register (4 and 5) may also be replaced by Color Select bits 0 and 1.

The palette may be changed very rapidly through use of this register.

Notes:
The Color Select register affects all of the palette registers. It works similarly to the segment/offset scheme of the CPU. You may select from four sets of 64 colors (Mode Control, index 10h, bit 7 set to 0), or 16 sets of 16 colors (Mode Control bit 7 set to 1).

This register does not affect mode 13h.

This register may be read from 3c1h.

BIOS Default Settings (all values are Hexadecimal):

Bits:
0–1   S_color 4-5
These bits replace bits 4 and 5 of the palette registers when the Attribute Mode Control register's bit 7 is set to 1 (see index 10h).

2–3   S_Color 6-7
These bits are used as the two most significant bits of the palette registers.

11

The Digital to Analog Converter Registers (VGA only)

The Digital to Analog Converter (DAC) registers convert binary color information from the VGA into analog signals for the monitor. Functionally, the DAC is very similar to the palette registers. The DAC contains 256 PEL data registers, each of which defines one color (this limits the VGA to a maximum of 256 accessible colors). Each PEL data register is 18 bits wide, using six bits for each primary color — red, green, and blue. Thus, the total number of definable colors is 262,144.

All mode 13h colors must be defined via the DAC PEL data registers. BIOS sets the first 16 mode 13h colors to match the other 16 color modes. The next 16 colors provide evenly varying shades of gray. The remaining 224 colors offer a wide variety of colors which should satisfy most user's needs. Because of the broad range of colors (and limited resolution) you probably will not redefine the DAC for mode 13h colors.

However, the remaining modes may use all 256 colors through the use of the Color Select register, index 14h of the Attribute register. Although a maximum of 16 may be displayed at one time, creative programming can make the DAC a powerful tool. For example, you could program the first 16 registers with shades of gray, and with each successive set of 16 colors, add color and gradually increase the intensity. You could then program a scene to change from a dark or cloudy setting into a brilliantly lit environment of vibrant colors, simply by incrementing the value of the Color Select register. Similarly, changing only two or three colors in each set could be used to produce simple animation effects such as snow, rain, or flashing lights (twinkling stars perhaps).

Port 3c7h: DAC State Register (VGA only)

Description: This register may be read to determine whether the DAC is in read or write mode. The DAC data register should be read by the CPU only while it is in read mode, and written only while in write mode.

Notes: This register is read-only.

Bits: 0–1   A value of 11b indicates the DAC is in write mode, and a value of 00b indicates read mode.

              2–7   Reserved

Port 3c7h: PEL Address Read Mode (VGA only)

Description: This register selects a PEL data register for reading (to write the PEL Data register, use the PEL Address Write Mode at port 3c8h). After selecting the PEL Data register, three six-bit values should be read from port 3c9h (the PEL Data register). The first read returns the red intensity; the second, green; and the third, blue.

Notes: This register is write-only.

              After reading the three color values, the PEL Address register will automatically increment to the next PEL Data register.

              If the read cycle is interrupted by another read or write request (rewriting either PEL Address register), the current cycle will be abandoned and will not affect the DAC color table.

              The read cycle should not be interrupted by writing the PEL Data register (the color table may be affected). However, the PEL Address register may be written at any time.

              The DAC State register may be used to determine the current mode of the DAC (read or write).

Interrupts should be disabled during the read cycle.

Reading or writing of successive PEL Data
registers must be separated by at least 240 nanoseconds.

Bits: 0–7   The PEL Data register (number 0-255)
                    to be read.

Port 3c8h: PEL Address Write Mode (VGA only)

Description: This register selects a PEL Data register for
writing (to read the PEL Data register, use the PEL Address Read Mode at port 3c7h). After selecting the PEL
Data register, three six-bit values should be written to
port 3c9h (the PEL Data register). The first value determines the red intensity; the second, green; and the
third, blue.

Notes: After writing the three color values, the PEL
Address register will automatically increment to the
next PEL Data register.

If the write cycle is interrupted by another read
or write request (rewriting either PEL Address register),
the current cycle will be abandoned and will not affect
the DAC color table.

The write cycle should not be interrupted by
reading the PEL Data register (the color table may be affected). However, the PEL Address register may be read
at any time.

The DAC State register may be used to determine
the current mode of the DAC (read or write).

Interrupts should be disabled during the write
cycle.

Reading or writing of successive PEL Data
registers must be separated by at least 240 nanoseconds.

Bits: 0–7   The PEL Data register (number 0-255)
                    to be written.

Port 3c9h: PEL Data Register (VGA only)

Description: This register reads or writes the current DAC color table values. Each cycle requires three sequential reads or writes at this address, consisting of three six bit color values — red, green, and blue, respectively.

Notes: If the read or write cycle is interrupted by another read or write request (rewriting either PEL Address register), the current cycle will be abandoned and will not affect the DAC color table.

You should not intermix read and write instructions. PEL Data register reads should be done in read mode only, and writes in write mode only.

The DAC State register may be used to determine the current mode of the DAC (read or write).

Interrupts should be disabled during the read or write cycle.

Reading or writing of successive PEL Data registers must be separated by at least 240 nanoseconds.

The PEL Data registers should not be read or written during the active display interval. The display should be blanked (see bit 5 of the Sequencer Clocking Mode register, port 3c5h index 1) or in the vertical retrace interval.

Bits: 0–5   The color value to be written or read.

6–7   Reserved

Port 3c6h: PEL Mask (VGA only)

Description: This register is initialized to ffh by BIOS whenever the video mode is changed. It should never be modified by any application program.

Notes: Attempting to modify this register could destroy the DAC color table.

Bits: 0–7   Reserved for internal use

12

The BIOS Save Area

Every time BIOS performs a mode reset, the registers are programmed to their default values for the selected mode and the default character set is reselected. Determining the default values is difficult since most of the EGA registers cannot be read. This can be very frustrating if your programs require mode switches or must run on a wide variety of configurations. Fortunately, the EGA BIOS sets up several areas in RAM to help circumvent problems associated with the EGA's mode switching behavior.

Memory address 0040:00a8h contains a pointer, called the Save Table Pointer, which points to a table (the save table) of eight double word pointers. When first initialized, the Save Table is located in the EGA BIOS, and its only entry points to the parameter table (unused pointers are set to 0000:0000). If you need to modify the save table, it should be copied from ROM to RAM. Then change the Save Pointer to address the new location. The contents of the save table are:

- Double word 1, the *Parameter Table Pointer*. This is the table which contains all of the default register settings. It includes some modes used internally by the EGA (modes 8-ch). The parameter table will be described in detail later. This table is the only save table entry required for the EGA's operation.
- Double word 2, the *Dynamic Save Area Pointer*. This entry can be set by the user to point to a 256-byte area in RAM called the Palette Save Area. When the mode is reset, the designated RAM area will be written with the palette register and overscan register settings (16 bytes, palette registers 0–15 followed by the overscan). The settings are simply copied from the parameter table, so you will probably find this function of little value.

- Double word 3, the *Alpha Mode Auxiliary Pointer*. This entry points to a table containing descriptors for an alphanumeric character set. During a mode reset, the ROM-based character generator is loaded into bit plane 2 of the EGA, and then the user-defined set is loaded if this entry is not set to 0000:0000. If the user-defined set is not defined as font table 0 (i.e., either font table 1–3), two font tables will exist after every alphanumeric mode set.
- Double word 4, the *Graphics Mode Auxiliary Pointer*. This entry points to a table containing descriptors for a graphics character set (it is similar to the Alpha Mode Auxiliary Pointer). If this entry is set to 0000:0000, the ROM character generator is used, otherwise the user defined set is used. Unlike the Alphanumeric Mode Auxiliary Pointer, only one font table may be defined.
- Double word 6 (VGA Only), the *Secondary Save Pointer*. The Secondary Save Pointer extends the address table for the VGA. Its structure and functions are similar to the Save Pointer.
- Double words 5–7 are not used on the EGA, and 6–7 are not used on the VGA.
- The Secondary Save Pointer has a more flexible structure than the original Save Pointer. The first word returns the table size, providing for future expansion.
- Double word 2, the *DCC Table Pointer*. This address points to a list of legal adapter combinations. It will typically exist in ROM for equipment checks when the system is started. This table is required for all systems which use the Secondary Save Pointer.
- Double word 3, the *Second Alpha Mode Auxiliary Pointer*. This entry points to a table containing descriptors for a secondary alphanumeric character set (extending the set to 512 characters). During a mode reset, this character set will be loaded into bit plane 2 along with the set selected via the Alpha Mode Auxiliary Pointer. Thus, systems using the secondary pointer may have 512 default user-defined characters (versus 256 user defined plus 256 ROM characters on the EGA). When set to 0000:0000, this entry will be ignored.
- Double word 4, the *User Palette Profile Table Pointer*. This points to a table of palette setting options. Normally, the attribute registers are set according to the Parameter Table, and the DAC registers are set according to internal ROM based values. You may override both (for selected modes) through the Palette Profile Table. When set to 0000:0000, this entry will be ignored.

The Parameter Table

The parameter table contains the settings for each video mode variation. Thus, mode 0 on a 200-line display has a separate entry from mode 0 on a 350-line display. Each mode entry is 64 bytes long and is organized as follows:

Offset	Size	Description
0	1 byte	Number of displayable columns
1	1 byte	Number of displayable rows
2	1 byte	Pixel height of the character cell
3	1 word	Memory per video pages (in bytes)

Sequencer Register Settings

5	1 byte	Clock Mode
6	1 byte	Map Mask
7	1 byte	Character Generator Select
8	1 byte	Memory Mode

Miscellaneous Register Settings

9	1 byte	Miscellaneous Register

CRTC Register Settings

ah	1 byte	Horizontal Total
bh	1 byte	Horizontal Display End
ch	1 byte	Start Horizontal Blanking
dh	1 byte	End Horizontal Blanking
eh	1 byte	Start Horizontal Retrace
fh	1 byte	End Horizontal Retrace
10h	1 byte	Vertical Total
11h	1 byte	Overflow
12h	1 byte	Preset Row Scan
13h	1 byte	Maximum Scan Line
14h	1 byte	Cursor Start
15h	1 byte	Cursor End
16h	1 byte	Unused
17h	1 byte	Unused
18h	1 byte	Unused
19h	1 byte	Unused
1ah	1 byte	Vertical Retrace Start
1bh	1 byte	Vertical Retrace End
1ch	1 byte	Vertical Display End
1dh	1 byte	Offset
1eh	1 byte	Underline Location
1fh	1 byte	Start Vertical Blanking

20h	1 byte	End Vertical Blanking
21h	1 byte	Mode Control
22h	1 byte	Line Compare

Attribute Register Settings:

23h	1 byte	Palette Register 0
24h	1 byte	Palette Register 1
25h	1 byte	Palette Register 2
26h	1 byte	Palette Register 3
27h	1 byte	Palette Register 4
28h	1 byte	Palette Register 5
29h	1 byte	Palette Register 6
2ah	1 byte	Palette Register 7
2bh	1 byte	Palette Register 8
2ch	1 byte	Palette Register 9
2dh	1 byte	Palette Register ah
2eh	1 byte	Palette Register bh
2fh	1 byte	Palette Register ch
30h	1 byte	Palette Register dh
31h	1 byte	Palette Register eh
32h	1 byte	Palette Register fh
33h	1 byte	Mode Control
34h	1 byte	Overscan Color
35h	1 byte	Color Plane Enable
36h	1 byte	Horizontal Panning

Graphics Controller Registers:

37h	1 byte	Set/Reset
38h	1 byte	Enable Set/Reset
39h	1 byte	Color Compare
3ah	1 byte	Data Rotate
3bh	1 byte	Read Map Select
3ch	1 byte	Mode Register
3dh	1 byte	Miscellaneous
3eh	1 byte	Color Don't Care
3fh	1 byte	Bit Mask

The parameter table settings of the cursor start and end registers in the high resolution alphanumeric modes use the compatibility setting — BIOS converts the eight-line setting to the equivalent 14- or 16-line register value.

The EGA parameter table has entries for 23 modes in the following order: 0–3 for CGA (200 line) modes, 4-eh, fh-10h when less than 64K is installed, fh-10h when more than 64K is installed, and 0–3 for ECD (350 line) modes. Note that modes 8-ch are included in the table even though they are not available (BIOS uses them internally). The VGA includes six additional entries for modes 0 and 1 (as one entry for VGA 40 column, 400 line alphanumeric modes), 2 and 3 (as one entry for VGA 80 column, 400 line alphanumeric modes), 7 (400 line alphanumeric monochrome), and 11h-13h.

The Alpha Mode Auxiliary Table

The Alphanumeric Auxiliary Table (addressed through the BIOS Save Area) defines defaults for a user-defined, memory-resident alphanumeric character set. These values (and the corresponding character set) are automatically loaded immediately following every mode set.

Offset	Size	Description
0	1 byte	Character size (scan lines) in font table
1	1 byte	Font table (0-3 EGA, 0-7 VGA)
2	1 word	Number of characters in the font table
4	1 word	First ASCII code defined by the font table
6	1 double word	Font table address (in first 640K RAM)
10	1 byte	Character size (scan lines) as used by the display. This may be different from offset 0, and BIOS will scale accordingly. If set to ffh, BIOS will use the largest possible character size.
11-?	1 byte	A list of all modes this character table supports. The last entry should be ffh to designate the end of the list.

The Secondary Alpha Mode Auxiliary Table is slightly different:

Offset	Size	Description
0	1 byte	Character size (scan lines) in font table
1	1 byte	Font Table (0-3 EGA, 0-7 VGA)
2	1 byte	Not Used
3	1 double word	Font table address (in first 640K RAM)
4-?	1 byte	A list of all modes this character table supports. The last entry should be ffh to designate the end of the list.

The Graphics Mode Auxiliary Table

The Graphics Mode Auxiliary Table (addressed through the BIOS Save Area) defines defaults for a user defined, memory-resident graphics mode character set. These values (and the corresponding character set) are automatically loaded immediately following every mode set.

Offset	Size	Description
0	1 byte	Character rows displayed on screen
1	1 word	Character size (scan lines) in font table
3	1 double word	Font table address
7-?	1 byte	A list of all modes this character table supports. The last entry should be ffh to designate the end of the list.

DCC Table

The DCC (Display Combination Code) Table lists the legal adapter pair combinations. Each adapter/display combination has a numeric code (its DCC): 0 = no display, 1 = MDA, 2 = CGA, 4 = Color EGA, 5 = Monochrome EGA, 6 = PGC (Professional Graphics Controller), 7 = Monochrome VGA, 8 = Color VGA. Each legal pair forms one entry (two bytes long). Thus an entry of 4,1 tells us that a Color EGA and MDA may co-exist without address conflicts.

Offset	Size	Description
0	1 byte	Number of Entries (Size = 2 * Entries + 4)
1	1 byte	Table Version Number
2	1 byte	Maximum Legal DCC
3	1 byte	Not Used
4–?	2 bytes	Entry 1 through Entry ?

User Palette Profile Table

The User Palette Profile Table allows you to customize both the Attribute Controller palette and DAC palette every time the mode is reset. Its operation is similar to that of the Auxiliary Tables, which modify the character sets. The Attribute register table is simply a list of byte values for each attribute register programmed. The DAC table uses three bytes per DAC register (one each for red, green, and blue).

Offset	Size	Desription
0	1 byte	Underlining flag (1 = always use underline, 0 = use the standard default, 0ffh = Never use underlining)
1	1 byte	Not Used
2	1 word	Not Used
4	1 word	Number of Attribute registers to set
6	1 word	First Attribute register to modify
8	1 double word	Address of Attribute register table
ch	1 word	Number of DAC registers to set
eh	1 word	First DAC register to modify
10h	1 double word	Address of DAC register table
14-?	1 byte	A list of all modes these palette tables support. The last entry should be ffh to designate the end of the list.

Additional BIOS RAM Areas

In addition to the tables and pointers, BIOS also stores two information bytes in segment 40h. The first byte (INFO) is located at offset 87h, and the second (INFO_3) at 88h. INFO has the following structure (from LSB to MSB):

Bit	Description
0	1 means that CGA cursor emulation is disabled (all references to cursor lines are taken literally)
1	1 means the EGA is using monochrome monitor
2	1 makes BIOS wait for a vertical retrace before performing certain functions (BIOS clears this bit to 0 after each usage)
3	1 means the EGA is not the active display
4	Not used
5-6	Installed memory 0=64k, 1=128K, 2=192K, and 3=256K
7	1 means the high bit was set on the last mode reset

INFO_3 has the following structure:

Bit	Description
0-3	Reflects the switch settings on the adapter card (primary and secondary displays)
4-7	Setting of the feature control bits (see the description of the Feature Control register)

Checking Display Type (BIOS Save Area) for All Adapters

There are several steps required to detect the type of display connected to the EGA. After the presence of the EGA has been established, you should find which display is active, since there may be more than one display adapter in the computer. This can be done by checking the equipment flag located at 0040:0010h. If bits 4 and 5 (30h) are set, a monochrome display is active. You should then determine whether the EGA is connected to a color or monochrome display. Function 10h of INT 10h is one way of returning this information (a value of 1 in BH denotes a monochrome monitor, 0 means a color monitor).

In many cases, simply knowing whether a monochrome or color monitor is attached is sufficient. However, if a color monitor is attached, you may want to determine whether it is an ECD. The display type should be read off the EGA's switches (this is the method used by the EGA BIOS). Again, function call 10h of INT 10h is useful for this purpose — the switch settings are returned in CL (note that CH contains the feature bit settings). If the switch settings are 3 or 9, an ECD is attached.

EGA Compatibles

The large numbers of EGA and VGA compatibles create several complications for programmers. Among the issues to be considered are whether to support extended modes, how compatible the various adapters are to the IBM implementation, and which adapter to use for application development.

Many manufacturers of EGA compatibles have extended the features of the EGA by emulating other adapters (such as the Hercules card), adding full CGA compatibility, and implementing autoswitch technology (to automatically select the proper adapter emulation). A large number of cards have actually expanded the definition of the EGA into higher resolution modes. Unfortunately, the various manufacturers use different techniques for using the expanded modes. Many are supplying drivers (or BIOS replacements) which emulate the VGA, and most programming concerns become a simple matter of addressing more memory. Note that a large number of the early VGA compatibles are really VGA BIOS compatibles (not register compatibles). You should write the manufacturer for specific programming details.

Sometimes, subtle timing differences between cards can make applications crash for no apparent reason — this is especially apparent during mode changes or programming several registers. Often, a simple delay will solve the problem. IBM recommends that successive accesses to the same I/O port be separated by a JMP SHORT $+2 instruction to allow the port time to recover on systems with fast processors. It is likely you will never need to resort to this method unless you use extensive register programming, but it is certainly something to bear in mind as a possible trouble spot (in many cases, timing problems can be alleviated by changing the order when a sequence of ports are used).

If possible, you should use either an IBM adapter or a compatible that uses the Chips and Technologies chip set for development work. BIOS compatibility is a fairly minor point — register compatibility is much more critical. The Chips and Technologies sets are very compatible with IBMs and are the most widely used (probably due to the low price). The primary advantage of the IBM adapter is the availability of ROM listings for $9.95 (part number 6280131 in the IBM Technical Directory, which can be ordered from IBM at (800) 426-7282). On a very few occasions, I have been able to find bugs in my programs by tracing through the interrupts while going through the ROM listings — something that is not possible with non-IBM adapters. Unfortunately, it is not possible with the VGA, since IBM no longer publishes ROM listings for its new products.

Using IBM adapters and testing on compatibles (the ideal approach) is often too expensive and time-consuming for hobbyists. If you are in the market for an EGA or VGA, your best bet is an adapter from a major manufacturer. In fact, you might want to try to get technical information on the adapter before ordering to find out whose technical staff is the most helpful and can provide the written documentation you may need.

13

Displays

Several types of displays are available for all of the various graphics systems on the market. You may want to consider issues beyond EGA compatibility when selecting a monitor. A better understanding of display hardware can help you make a good choice and can also improve your understanding of the adapter. Several factors influence the quality of a display, including the interface type (composite, digital, or analog), the scanning speed, and the dot pitch; some of these factors are interrelated. We will begin with a discussion of the interface and then trace through the beam's path, introducing factors as they become relevant.

The CGA supports either a composite or RGB monitor. The composite monitor receives an analog signal like that used for televisions. Composite signals are formed by combining the red, green, and blue signals (along with synchronization information) at the adapter and then separating the signals at the monitor. The advantage of a single signal is that it can be transmitted over a single cable. While this may work well for broadcasting purposes, the problems of accurately separating the color information limits the resolution. Composite monitors are not directly supported by the EGA.

RGB monitors receive the signals for red, green, and blue on different lines. The Color Display and ECD are digital RGB monitors, which simply means that each pin on the connector is either on or off. The original IBM Color Display used three pins for the colors, and a fourth pin to select intensity. The Enhanced Color Displays use six pins (two for each color). One pin for each color signals a low-intensity beam, and the other signals a medium-intensity beam. Both can be combined to form a high-intensity beam, giving four intensities (including off) for each color. With three colors in four intensities, a total of 64 colors (4 x 4 x 4) are possible. Note that the IBM monochrome

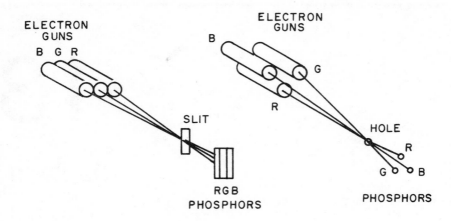

Figure 13-1 Electron gun arrangements

monitor uses the same technique as an RGB, but it has only one pin for single color, and one pin for intensity. With digital monitors, increasing the number of available colors requires increasing the number of pins.

With the introduction of the Personal System/2 series of computers, IBM announced analog RGB monitors. Like digital RGB monitors, the red, green, and blue signals are transmitted on separate lines. However, the intensity of each signal is controlled by the voltage on each line, and thus only three lines are necessary. When large numbers of colors are required, the connector for an analog RGB monitor is much simpler than for a digital monitor. The number of displayable colors on an analog monitor is essentially infinite — limited by the adapter's ability to generate different voltages, and your eyes' ability to distinguish different intensities.

Composite and RGB define only the interface between the adapter and the display. Beyond the interface, there are several methods for creating displayed image. All standard PC monitors use a raster-scan display to create the image. In a raster-scan display, the position of three electron beams (one for monochrome displays) is continually sweeping across the surface of the tube. The tube's surface is coated with phosphors that glow when struck by electrons (and for a short time thereafter), and, of course, each beam may be turned on in order to light a phosphor or off to leave it black.

A color monitor's phosphors may be arranged in one of two ways — in-line or triad (See Figure 13-1). A triad consists of red, green, and blue phosphor dots (and three electron guns) arranged as a triangle. An in-line system uses red, green, and blue phosphor vertical lines (and the three electron guns) arranged horizontally. The triad is the most common arrangement. A mask between the phosphors and the

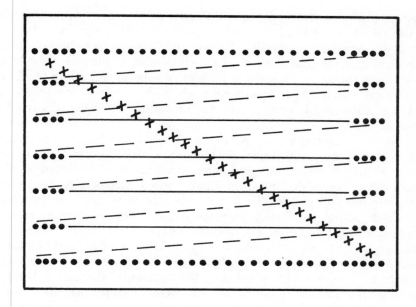

ACTIVE DISPLAY AREA
OVER SCAN
HORIZONTAL RETRACE (BLANKING)
VERTICAL RETRACE (BLANKING)

Figure 13-2 Simplified scan diagram

electron guns allows each gun to illuminate only one color of phosphor when the guns are properly aligned.

The electron beam scans the phosphor-coated screen from left to right and top to bottom. The period during which the beams return to the left is known as the horizontal retrace. During most of the retrace, the guns must be turned off to prevent writing in the active display area (the area which contains the actual character and/or graphics data); this is known as horizontal blanking. The area immediately surrounding the display area, in which the beam may be turned on during the retrace interval, is called the overscan (or border). The active display area is the portion of the screen that contains characters and/or graphics. These components of the scan are shown in simplified form in Figure 13-2.

During the horizontal display interval, the frequency with which the beam can be turned on and off (the dot clock frequency) determines the horizontal resolution of the adapter. It is fairly easy to increase the horizontal resolution simply by increasing the dot clock rate, and several of the EGA-compatible cards implement 132 column modes through this method. Of course, the display must have a small enough phosphor dot so that the different pixels can be seen. The size of the triad; i.e., the size of the hole in the mask, is known as the dot pitch. Generally, the smaller the dot pitch, the better the quality of the display. Note that the actual phosphor size is not directly related to the pixel size. A pixel could consist of several phosphor triads or vice versa. Often, the area around a white character or pixel may appear reddish, bluish, or greenish, because only a fraction of a triad is illuminated.

After a horizontal scan has been completed, the beam is moved to the next line during the horizontal retrace (this applies to noninterlaced monitors; televisions and some monitors are interlaced so that every other line is displayed, and two vertical passes are required to complete one full image). This sequence continues until the last line, at which point the vertical retrace begins. The vertical retrace is similar to the horizontal retrace; the electron guns may be enabled through a small overscan area and then turned off (vertical blanking) as the beam returns to the top left corner of the screen. The vertical resolution depends on two rates — the horizontal frequency and the vertical frequency. Higher horizontal sweep frequencies allow more lines to be displayed during each vertical cycle. Likewise, a longer vertical interval (lower vertical frequency) allows more horizontal lines to be displayed. However, if the vertical frequency becomes too low, the display will flicker. Most people can detect flicker when the rate drops below 60 Hz, and thus most displays use vertical frequencies of about 60 Hz (the monochrome display is 50 Hz, the ECD is 60 Hz, and the PS/2 displays vary between 60 and 70 Hz).

Most monitors can tolerate some variation in horizontal and vertical frequencies. Several manufacturers sell displays that will automatically adjust to wide variations in frequencies. These multisynchronous displays help ensure that future adapters with higher frequencies will work with the monitors. Of course, there are no guarantees; a monitor designed for a digital interface does not adapt well to analog usage, since it is not capable of generating all of the possible colors (without modifying the interface). It is fairly simple to convert a digital signal to an analog equivalent, so a multisynchronous analog display is the most flexible option at this time.

The entire display must be scanned rapidly enough that the image does not flicker. As the scan rate increases, more pixels may be displayed during a given time interval, thereby increasing the resolution. ECDs support two scan rates: 15.75 kHz (the same as the standard color display) and 21.8 kHz. Several multiscan monitors are available that match their scan rate to that of the display adapter. Many of these displays have a maximum scan rate in the 30 kHz range, supporting resolutions up to about 900 x 550. In some cases, a slower scan rate is used with long persistence phosphors. Long-persistence phosphors glow for a longer time after being struck by the electrons and thus do not flicker with lower scan rates, but they tend to make the screen hard to read during scrolling. The monochrome display is a good example of a monitor that uses a long-persistence phosphor, although some companies use long-persistence phosphors in color displays.

The CPU is usually given access to the display memory during the vertical and horizontal retrace periods, and the CRT is given access during the actual scan. If the CPU writes memory while the CRT is reading, snow will appear on the screen. The EGA's Sequencer registers control CRT and CPU memory access to prevent such conflicts from occurring. In fact, the Sequencer will even allow the CPU to write during the scan when the CRT is not accessing memory. During a scan in the high-resolution modes, the CRT has access to memory for four of every five cycles, and the CPU has access during the remaining cycle. This scheme prevents the CPU from writing at its fastest speed, but it is faster and more efficient than waiting for the retrace.

When selecting a color monitor, you should first decide whether you need an analog or digital. Then you should select between a multisynchronous or fixed scan rate monitor. After selecting the type of monitor, it is important to examine the quality — especially if you will be using the monitor for extended periods. How clearly are the characters formed at your typical viewing distance (and are they large enough for you)? Do room and window lights glare off the screen (many screens have an etched surface to prevent glare)? Are the colors true? Colors are perhaps the trickiest aspect, since individual tastes vary widely. Try experimenting with different settings. You should also use your software to examine the colors in both alphanumeric and graphics modes, since they are sometimes different (especially if some of your programs change the palette).

14

Programming Tricks and Traps

Modifying the EGA BIOS Interrupt

Portions of the EGA BIOS make use of recursive calls — some of these recursions only occur in rare circumstances. One example of this is the alternate font-loading routine. When an alternate font is loaded, a mode reset is performed via a function call to INT 10h. When writing programs that add functions to such routines, it may be important to trace these iterations (especially if your routines must run after the original call; e.g., to fix bugs in the ROM). One method for doing this follows: create a memory variable with an initial value of 0, increment the variable before calling the original ROM routines, and decrement the variable each time the routine is exited. Call your routine only if the variable is 0 (unless it is important to make your call every time, in which case you should build an internal stack).

```
add        recur,1
pushf
call       old_int10
sub        recur,1
cmp        recur,0
jne        skip_new
call       new_routine
skip_new:  iret
```

Using Write Modes 0 and 2

When programming graphics for direct memory access, it is often more efficient to use mode 2, which is not supported by BIOS (see the description of the Mode register for more information). However, it is important to switch back to mode 0 after the plotting routines have finished, because BIOS will not write to the screen correctly while in mode one or two. It is also important to restore any other EGA registers that may have been modified (such as the Bit Mask register).

Debugging mode one or two graphics routines can be very difficult on a single monitor system. Therefore, it is wise to develop your routines using mode 0 and modify the routines to use mode 2 after the major portions of the routines have been debugged. Also, it is very helpful to place the plotting and mode setting routines in macros or subroutines for easy and complete modification of all affected code.

Store and Restore Modified States

Your programs should always set the cursor and underline locations in order to deal with some peculiarities on the EGA (see the discussion of alternate font tables below). You would be wise to store the original settings at the beginning of your program and then restore the settings at the end (this is especially important for programs which may be run from within another application, such as a word processor or database). This should be done with all programs (not just EGA applications), since it affects software written for the CGA or monochrome adapter which is running on the EGA.

Restoring Modes — Make Sure to Clear the High Bit

In addition to saving and restoring the cursor and underline locations, you should also save and restore the display mode. This is especially important if you will be setting the mode during your program (this is also a good practice, as I have seen several programs that assume that the display is in text mode when they are started, and write garbage to the screen if another application has switched the display to graphics mode). The main thing to watch for is the high bit of the mode number.

When setting the mode on the EGA, some programs set bit 7 in order to leave the display memory undisturbed (for example, a memory resident program can leave the graphics memory intact while switching to text mode, or change the character set without redrawing the screen). If your program stores the original mode and the original mode had the high bit set, strange things may happen when you restore the original mode (sometimes the display will completely blank out or garbage characters will appear). Because of this, it is a good idea to clear the high bit before restoring the original mode (AND mode,7fh will do this).

Saving the state of the EGA when switching modes can be complicated by two factors. First, each time the mode is switched to alphanumeric, the font tables are loaded into bit plane 3. When switching back to graphics mode, bit plane 3 may be filled with seemingly random dots (which usually appear as red against a black background). This could be avoided by using an unused display page or by saving the contents of bit plane 3 (which would be slow and wasteful of memory). Second, the contents of the latch registers will be lost. This is of special importance when one program may interrupt another. The latch registers should be saved to an unused area just beyond the last displayable address (this can be done using write mode 1; see the description of the Graphics Controller Mode register).

Presence Test

There are several ways to detect the presence of an EGA. Perhaps the easiest test is to check the ROM latch at C000:0000h (the location of the EGA ROM). The BIOS searches for extensions to the existing ROM by checking for the value aa55h in the sections of memory reserved for ROM, and your programs can do the same thing. However, the PS/2 BIOS does not use C000:0000h, and this method should be avoided.

A much better method requests BIOS functions which are unique to VGA or EGA configurations. First, set BX to 0, and use BIOS call 1ah to return the active (and installed but inactive) adapter type. If BL is 7, a monochrome VGA is active, and if BL is 8, a color VGA is active (other values may be returned; see the description of function call 1ah). If BIOS call 1ah is not supported by the system, BX will remain set to 0.

If function 1ah is not supported, move down to a BIOS call supported by the EGA. Since function call 12h is unique to the EGA (at this stage), and it returns information about the EGA that may be useful to your program, it is usually the ideal choice. BL must be set to 10h to return the EGA information — it will return a code for installed memory if the EGA is installed. Therefore, if BL remains set to 10h, an EGA is not installed (if installed, the value will be between 0 and 3).

The following program demonstrates the basic approach (the program will print the active EGA or VGA configuration). Note that if a VGA were installed as a secondary adapter, it would not be reported — this could be checked through register BH after function call 1ah.

```
cr          equ      13

lf          equ      10

B_RAM       segment at 40h
            org      87h
                        info      db      ?

B_RAM       ends

data        segment public
                        no_support      db      'The required EGA or VGA
                                                    is not '
                                        db      'active',cr,lf
                        clr_ega         db      'You have an active color
                                                    EGA',cr,lf
                        clr_vga         db      'You have an active color
                                                    VGA',cr,lf
                        mono_ega        db      'You have an active
                                                    monochrome '
                                        db      'EGA',cr,lf
                        mono_vga        db      'You have an active
                                                    monochrome '
                                        db      'VGA',cr,lf

data        ends

code        segment public
                        assume CS:code

main        proc     far

start:      push     DS
            sub      AX,AX
            push     AX

            mov      AX,data
            mov      DS,AX
            assume   DS:data

            mov      AX,1a00h   ;function 1a return
                                display code
            int      10h        ;AL will return as 1a
                                if supported

            cmp      AL,1ah
            jne      no_dc
```

```
        cmp     BL,7        ;is it a monochrome VGA?
        je      mono_v

        cmp     BL,8        ;is it a color VGA?
        je      color_v

        mov     BL,4        ;is it a color EGA?
        je      color_e

        mov     BL,5        ;is it a monochrome EGA
        je      mono_e


no_dc:
        mov     AH,12h      ;Get information
        mov     BL,10h      ;about the EGA
        int     10h
        cmp     BL,10h      ;did it come back as
                            ;10h (no EGA)?
        je      invalid     ; yes, skip next test

        push    DS
        mov     AX,B_RAM
                            ;BIOS RAM area
        mov     DS,AX
        assume  DS:B_RAM
        mov     BL,info     ;get information byte

        pop     DS
        assume  DS:DATA

        test    BL,8        ;is the EGA active
        jz      valid       ; bit 3 = 0 means EGA active

invalid:
        mov     BX,offset no_support
        jmp     finish

valid:
        cmp     BH,1        ;is monitor type monochrome?
        je      mono_e
        jmp     color_e

mono_v:
        mov     BX,offset mono_vga
        jmp     finish
```

```
color_v:
            mov     BX,offset clr_vga
            jmp     finish

color_e:
            mov     BX,offset clr_ega
            jmp     finish

mono_e:
            mov     BX,offset mono_ega
            jmp     finish

finish:
            call    print_msg

            ret

main        endp

print_msg   proc    near

next_char:
            mov     dl,[bx]         ;put it in dl
            mov     ah,2            ;write to screen

            int     21h             ;DOS call

            inc     bx
            cmp     dl,10           ;line feed?
            jne     next_char       ;no, get next character

            ret

print_msg   endp

code        ends

end         start
```

Problems With Using Alternate Font Tables

Using alternate loadable font tables disables the underline attribute in mode 7, and makes the cursor disappear on the ECD in modes 0–3. Unfortunately, this causes problems for word processors that work with alternate characters and show underlining on the monochrome monitor. These complications trace back to the EGA BIOS.

When alternate fonts are used in monochrome mode, the BIOS tries to set the underline to the bottom line of the character box — however, it uses the length of the box (l) as the location, rather than the l-1 (keep in mind that line numbers begin with 0). Thus, a character 14 dots high gets an underline on line 14, when it should really be on line 13. The problem can be solved by setting the underline location register to the correct value after every mode reset. Note that this is not a problem with the parameter table — the Alphanumeric Auxiliary Mode Pointer overrides the parameter table setting.

The disappearance of the cursor on the ECD is also a result of the BIOS programming. In order to maintain compatibility with the CGA, BIOS operations in modes 0–3 always behave as if the character box is eight lines long (even though it is 14 lines on the ECD). As in the monochrome alternate character routines, the location of the cursor line is based on the length of the character box (but correctly accounts for the l-1 numbering system). However, during a mode reset this routine does not account for the apparent "shortening" of the character box, and sets the cursor location to lines 12–13, rather than lines 7–8. Note that the set cursor BIOS call (function call 1) still accounts for the shortened box — it is only the internal routine during the mode reset that does not.

To deal with these problems, you should always set the cursor and underline locations in your programs (including programs not specifically designed for the EGA). And it would also be wise to store the original values at the beginning of your programs, so that you can restore them at the end.

Vertical Interrupts

Most standard EGA operations may take place at any time, unlike some adapters, which require all I/O be done during retrace intervals. However, there are some operations, such as those which deal with attributes, which should be done only during a vertical retrace. Also, some screen writing functions will look much better if done during the vertical retrace. For example, the screen may flicker during animation if objects are erased and rewritten while the electron beam is scanning the object — writing the object to memory during the retrace ensures that the CRT will not be accessing the same memory locations. Note that this flickering effect is not the same as "snow" produced on some adapter cards when the CRT and CPU access the same data area. A final advantage of using the vertical interrupt deals with display timing. Since the CRT's timing is roughly the same for all PCs (50–70 Hz), the vertical retrace provides a built-in "clock" for screen updates. You can make the screen scroll or move objects at a fairly fixed rate from one type of machine to another.

There are two methods for determining the vertical retrace status: Use IRQ2 to inform the program of the vertical interrupt, or use a loop to check the status. The AT and PS/2's hardware actually uses IRQ9 (rather than IRQ2), but it is redirected to IRQ2 for software compatibility. The primary advantages of using IRQ2 are that it provides a routine that is independent of the main program (the program does not need to stop and wait for the vertical retrace), and execution always begins at the start of the vertical retrace (assuming the EGA routine is the first in the chain). However, using IRQ2 is very awkward and you may find it is not worth the extra trouble. Also, a few EGA compatibles do not implement IRQ2 correctly, and the IBM VGA adapter for PCs and ATs does not support hardware interrupts. Writing a program that waits for the vertical retrace is much easier, but the retrace status indicates only that the vertical retrace is in progress; it may be almost finished when you first check. You can get around this by first waiting for a display interval and then waiting for the vertical retrace.

What makes using an interrupt routine so awkward? You must provide the interrupt routine with status information; e.g., whether to scroll the display one pixel. You must make sure the IRQ2 was generated by the graphics adapter, since other adapters may also use IRQ2. The Vertical Retrace End register, which enables IRQ2 checking, also controls the timing of the end of the vertical retrace. Since the Vertical Retrace End register is a write-only register on the EGA (fortunately, the VGA can read its contents) the program must retrieve the correct value from the parameter table, unless you can guarantee the mode will not change. The interrupt being processed must be cleared and reenabled through the Vertical Retrace End register, and the interrupt controller must be told to allow further interrupts when the routine is finished (this is called the EOI, End of Interrupt, and is done by sending the value 20h to port 20h — it is not required on the PS/2 family). Finally, the routine usually needs to complete its operation(s) before the end of the vertical retrace. You might also want to disable interrupts while the vertical retrace routine is in effect. Otherwise, another interrupt request might delay the processing of the current interrupt.

Also, a few of the EGA compatibles have problems with their IRQ2 implementation. Some cards have the status bit reversed (see bit 7 of Input Status Register Zero). Other cards do not correctly implement the Clear Vertical Interrupt (bit 4 of the Vertical Retrace End register). Normally, the current interrupt is cleared by writing 0, and then reenabled by writing 1 (this is not really necessary for edge triggered interrupts used by the PC and AT, but is required for the level sensing interrupts used by the Micro Channel).

The example program, VERTIRQ2, demonstrates the use of IRQ2 for detecting the vertical interrupt. The program alternately places a line of spaces and then a line of V's on the upper two lines of the screen. The first line is printed only during the vertical retrace; the second line is printed as fast as the computer can loop through the routine. If you run this program, notice how the first line appears as a steady image, while the second flickers.

This program is quite simple, and it demonstrates several notable points. First, if you are not familiar with hardware interrupt handlers, the IRQ2 routine occupies INT 0ah of the interrupt vector table (IRQ0-IRQ7 use INT 8-INT 0fh, respectively). Second, this program will not work reliably without its own stack. VERTIRQ2 chains to the DOS-based EOI routine, which sets a stack segment if the application does not provide one, and the stack DOS creates may conflict with the application's code and data segments (the DOS EOI routine is not the same as the BIOS routine listed in the Technical Reference, since DOS must provide a latch at each interrupt for device drivers). Third, when the program finishes, the final clearing of the interrupt (via the BIOS mode set) causes an interrupt. You should make sure the program can handle this last request.

Fourth, note the overhead required to process the hardware interrupt. Of course, some overhead could be reduced by requiring the program to run only in certain modes, branching out of the routine if the mode number was not legal or omitting the mode check under the assumption that the mode will not change. Overhead could be further reduced by ignoring other IRQ2 routines (not a very good practice, since some hardware may be disabled — especially on the AT, which chains eight additional interrupts, including the hard disk, onto IRQ2). If you choose to ignore other IRQ2 routines, be sure to restore INT 0ah to its original value when the program ends. Fourth, the program enables IRQ2 at the programmable interrupt controller (port 21h) and saves the previous setting for restoration at the end.

Despite the complications of using IRQ2, you can implement functions that would be extremely difficult to emulate without true hardware interrupts. This is especially true of TSR applications — for example, IRQ2 would be handy for creating a flashing, graphics mode cursor. Or you could also write a real-time clock to update the time in the corner of the screen on every vertical retrace. TSR applications may interfere with programs which check the status of the vertical retrace via Status Register One, since the status bit indicates every IRQ2, even those from other devices, when the EGA IRQ2 is enable (see the description of Input Status Register One, bit 3).

Standard applications may also benefit from the use of Interrupt routines. An IRQ2 animation routine could share a data area with the main program, updating the screen during every vertical retrace. This would free the application to handle calculations and keyboard input without having to wait for the vertical retrace during every loop (potentially improving the routine's performance if the screen is constantly changing). If you are really ambitious, you could also write a keyboard interrupt handler (IRQ1/INT 9). Or a flashing graphics cursor or real-time clock could be programmed for your application only (eliminating the problem of interference with other standard applications).

The period from the end of the vertical display to the end of the vertical total for the highest resolution modes is very short (.64 milliseconds) compared to the 200 line modes (3.9 ms) and does not allow enough time to perform much graphics manipulation on 4.77-MHz PCs. However, it is possible to work around some problems. For example, the vertical retrace routine could be further divided into multiple routines, which would run every nth vertical interrupt. Or draw images that always appear near the bottom screen last — this gives a little extra time after the end of the vertical interrupt and before the electron beam reaches the bottom of the display area (make sure operations that must be done during the retrace interval, such as changing the palette, are done at the beginning of the routine).

As you can see, writing an interrupt routine can be very complicated, and debugging interrupt routines can be extremely difficult. It is almost impossible to trace a hardware interrupt routine because it may be invoked at any time. It is extremely important that all registers that are modified by the interrupt handler are returned to their initial values at the end of the routine. If you are doing much interrupt programming, you might want to consider purchasing a good hardware-assisted debugger.

If possible, you should first write and debug the routine outside the interrupt handler, and then place the finished routine within the interrupt handler. You could also write the routine as a soft interrupt routine at a different interrupt vector (INT 60h — INT 67h are reserved for user applications such as this) and later change the vector to ah and implement the hardware interrupt features.

A typical development cycle may look like this:

Write the program as a continuous loop, including a call to the screen handler. The screen handling subroutine should wait for the vertical retrace, checking first for the display interval and then the retrace so as to get the beginning of the interval (see the VERTINT program). The subroutine should restore all registers to their original contents — although this is not strictly necessary, it will help with the conversion later. Finally, limit the subroutine to functions necessary for the display. Unrelated functions (such as calculating an object's position, keyboard input, etc.) should be left in the main program. You may discover that your program works without the IRQ2 routine. If so, you certainly save a lot of work and frustration.

When the screen handling routine is working properly, set it up as a software interrupt at 60h. Now you can confirm that the interrupt call and return has been implemented properly. You might want to write a second INT 60h routine, which would be installed first to test chaining from your routine to the "original" routine. You can also make sure the "original" routine is restored properly. At this stage, you will still be able to trace through the interrupt with a software debugger.

Finally, change the interrupt to 0ah — remember to program the interrupt controller to respond to IRQ2 (and restore it to its original state at the end of the program). Everything should work now, and you will probably not discover any further bugs — at least nothing difficult to trace.

There are a few things worth noting in the VERTINT program. VERTINT has many fewer program loops than VERTIRQ2 (the outer loop has been entirely eliminated). VERTINT will run the same speed on all computers, because it is limited to one loop per vertical retrace. On my AT, both VERTINT and VERTIRQ2 end after about 16 seconds. However, VERTIRQ2 will take much longer on a standard PC and will finish earlier on a faster machine, since the looping routine is not limited by the vertical retrace. Also, note that only the very end of the second line of V's flashes in VERTINT (on a fast enough computer); the retrace routine does not use the entire vertical retrace interval, so most of the second line, which prints almost immediately after the first, is also written during the vertical interrupt.

A program's performance for either vertical retrace method can be greatly increased by limiting updates to areas which have changed. If an area of the display has not changed, there is no point in rewriting it. You could also develop an algorithm that updates as many changed areas as possible in one retrace, and finishes the remaining areas during later retraces, but the overhead and difficulty of programming such a routine would probably make it impractical for most situations.

Smooth Scrolling

Vertical retrace detection is also useful for smooth scrolling applications. In addition to Input Status Register One, the EGA provides several registers to support smooth scrolling. However, the application program must assume a great deal of the overhead associated with smooth scrolling, and the method varies slightly between graphics and alphanumeric applications. The following registers are all useful for implementing pixel scrolling, and you may want to refer back to their descriptions:

CRTC registers
    Start Address registers
    Preset Row Scan register
    Offset register
    End Horizontal Retrace register (EGA only)
Graphics Controller
    Mode register

Attribute register
  Horizontal PEL Pan register

The program SMOOTH.ASM is an example of smooth scrolling in alphanumeric mode (graphics mode scrolling is slightly easier). To effectively implement smooth scrolling, the adapter must create a logical display page which is larger than the actual display. This is easily accomplished by setting the Offset register, which directly controls the virtual width. The Start Address register is then set to the first displayable character, usually below and to the right of the first character on the virtual page. The bottom of the virtual page is at the end of the adapter's addressable memory, unless you will be using multiple pages, in which case it would be the row before the start of the next page.

Scrolling left and right works the same in both alphanumeric and graphics modes. To scroll the display right, the Horizontal Pel Pan register starts at 0 (except for 9 dot alphanumeric modes, which start at 8 and goes to 0 on the next scroll), and increments by one on each vertical retrace. To scroll faster, you could scroll more than one pixel per retrace; to go slower, wait for multiple retraces before scrolling. Upon reaching 7 (3 for 256-color mode), the Start Address register is incremented by one, and the Pel Pan register is set back to 0 (or 8 for 9 dot modes). The procedure is reversed to scroll left: first the Start Address is decremented, and the Pel Pan register is set to 7 (or 3). The Pel Pan register is then decremented until the full character width has been finished.

The procedure must be modified slightly if the memory is chained. The only chained BIOS video modes 7 and 10h on EGAs with less than 64K, but you could create your own chained modes on either the EGA or VGA (in fact, the VGA can chain up to four planes to act as one). Since the shift registers load 16 pixels (or possibly 32 on the VGA) instead of 8, all 16 bits must be shifted before changing the Start Address. The Pel Pan register does not support such operation, so the EGA provides an extra bit in the End Horizontal Retrace register, and the VGA provides two extra bits in the Preset Row Scan register. The Pel Pan register continues an eight-pixel cycle, but instead of incrementing the Start Address after the first cycle, the End Horizontal Retrace register is changed.

Vertical scrolling is almost identical to horizontal scrolling. In alphanumeric modes, the Preset Row Scan register is incremented (or decremented) in place of the Horizontal PEL Pan register. The Start Address changes are made at the limits of the Preset Row Scan register (usually 0 and 7, 13, or 15). Also, the Start Address is changed by twice the value of the Offset register setting (to get to the next line, rather than the next character). Graphics modes can skip setting the Preset Row Scan register, since each "line" of memory is only one pixel high. You simply add (or subtract) twice the value of the Offset register to scroll to the next row of pixels.

While the scrolling sequence is fairly simple, proper timing is essential, and can be a bit tricky. Using the Horizontal Pel Pan register is fairly easy; you need only wait for the vertical retrace, and then change the setting. However, the Start Address register should be changed only during the display interval (it will not take effect until the start of the following vertical retrace interval). When the Pel Pan register's limit is reached, the Start Address should be changed first (during the display interval), and then the Horizontal Pel Panning register (during the vertical retrace).

The timing method will work with the Preset Row Scan register. However, the Technical Reference recommends that the Preset Row Scan also be changed during the display interval. Essentially, it may be programmed at any time since it only takes effect at the beginning of the display interval. However, the Preset Row Scan will implement a new value any time during the display of the first scan line, and the display will jump one line if it is changed during this time. If you program the Preset Row Scan register during the display interval, wait for a horizontal retrace (see bit 0 of Input Status Register One, port 3?ah).

Chapter

15

Applications

Graphics Routines

Graphics applications usually require four fundamental operations —
writing characters to the screen, plotting individual points, drawing
lines, and drawing ellipses. Writing characters and plotting points are
trivial, and drawing lines is not too difficult because the equations are
linear (many people use the well-known Bresenham's algorithm for
drawing lines). Drawing circles or ellipses requires more computation
because of the squared terms, hence the equations are more difficult
to implement and take longer to solve than those for lines. At first
glance, it would seem real number operations are required for
evaluating square roots. However, an integer technique similar to
Bresenham's line algorithm can be used.

Bresenham's algorithm exploits the grid arrangement of pixels,
which are always represented as integer coordinates. By avoiding
floating point computations, the microprocessor's integer routines can
be used to create a high-speed plotting routine. Given a line (or curve)
lying on a grid, the algorithm chooses which point lies closest to the
line. First, you choose a starting point and a direction of movement
(up, down, left, or right). Each time the cursor moves one unit in the
chosen direction, the algorithm determines whether to adjust the position one unit in the perpendicular direction. Note that this method
can move a maximum of one step in the perpendicular direction for
each step in the selected direction — the slope is limited to 45 degrees.
Let's see how this works for Bresenham's line algorithm.

The Line Algorithm

Start with the equation for a line, $y = mx + b$. Note that the slope, m, is simply the change in the y direction divided by the change in the x direction, $m = y/x$. Both y and x are easily obtained from the endpoints of the line, (x_a, y_a) and (x_b, y_b); $y = y_b - y_a$ and $x = x_b - x_a$. For this derivation, we will assume the slope lies between 0 and 1 in the first quadrant. We will start with an arbitrary point on the line, (x_n, y_n), and move to the right one pixel at a time until we reach the last point, (x_m, y_m). The pixel resolution of the display forces us to integer values for x_n, but the actual y_n value usually is not an integer. We will choose y_n so that the value is either exact, or the closest integer less than the exact value. Since we are moving up the y axis, we know that y_n will either be the same as the value we selected ($y_n = y_n$) or one larger ($y_n = y_n + 1$). By selecting consecutive, relative pixel locations, the line will be made as smooth as possible, and the final algorithm will be independent of the display resolution. The y coordinate may not be the exact position of the "true" line, since we are limited to the pixel resolution of the physical display, so we will call the actual value y and express the difference between the "true" and two trial locations as:

$d_1 = y_n - y$, and
$d_2 = y - (y_n + 1)$.

The difference (d_1 or d_2) will be smallest for the point (y_n+1 or y_n) which lies closest to the actual point, y. We will use the difference of the differences as a test parameter; i.e., $t = d_1 - d_2$. The sign of the test parameter is used to select the appropriate case. Note that there are four possibilities:

case	d_1	d_2	t_n	choose
1) $y_n >= y$ and $y_n + 1 > y$	+s	$-g$	+	y_n
2) $y_n >= y$ and $y_n + 1 > y$	-s	$-g$	+	y_n
3) y_n and $y_n + 1 >= y$	-g	$-s$	$-$	y_n+1
4) $y_n < y$ and $y_n + 1 >= y$	-g	$+s$	$-$	y_n+1

g = greater absolute value, s = smaller absolute value.

When the sign of the test parameter is positive we choose y_n, and when negative, y_n+1.

Now, express the test equation in terms of y

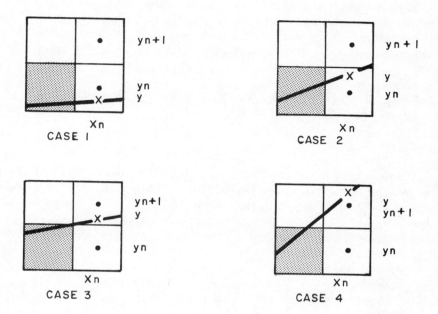

Figure 15-1 Four closest fit possibilities for a line

$t_n =$
$d_1 - d_2 =$
$y_n - y - [y - (y_n+1)] =$
$y_n - y - y + y_n + 1 =$
$2y_n - 2y + 1 =$

and substitute the line equation $y = x \, y/x + b$ into the test equation. Note that x_n is always known.

$t_n = 2y_n - 2(x_n)y/x - 2b + 1.$

This gives t for any point, and we will apply it to the starting point to get t_1, i.e. $t_1 = 2y_1 - 2(y/x)x_1 - 2b + 1$, where $b = y_1 - (y/x)x_1$. This obviously reduces to $t_1 = 1$. It is a positive value, so we place it at (x_1, y_1), which makes sense. However, the equation is not too useful, since it gives us the location of a point we have already placed. What we really need is t for the next point, t_{n+1}.

$t_{n+1} =$
$2y_{n+1} - 2(y/x)x_{n+1} - 2b + 1 =$
$2y_{n+1} - 2(y/x)(x_n+1) - 2b + 1$

Rather than computing the next test value in terms of x and y, which makes the equations more complex and no more useful than the original, we will express the new test value in terms of the previous test value. So, subtracting the previous result, t_n from t_{n+1}:

$$t_{n+1} - t_n =$$
$$2y_{n+1} - 2(y/x)(x_n+1) - 2b + 1 - [2y_n - 2(y/x)x_n - 2b + 1] =$$
$$2y_{n+1} - 2y_n - 2(y/x)(x_n+1) + 2(y/x)x_n - 2b + 2b + 1 - 1 =$$
$$2y_{n+1} - 2y_n + 2y/x(-x_n - 1 + x_n) =$$
$$2y_{n+1} - 2y_n - 2y/x$$

We now have a factor which can be added to the current test value to get the next test value, i.e., $t_n + (t_{n+1} - t_n) = t_{n+1}$. The term y_{n+1} may take one of two values, either y_n (for $t_{n+1} > 0$) or y_{n+1} (for $t_{n+1} < 0$).

For $y_{n+1} = y_n$:
$$t_{n+1} - t_n =$$
$$2y_n - 2y_n - 2y/x =$$
$$-2y/x$$
$$t_{n+1} = t_n - 2y/x$$
For $y_{n+1} = y_n + 1$:
$$t_{n+1} - t_n =$$
$$2y_n + 2 - 2y_n - 2y/x =$$
$$2 - 2y/x$$
$$t_{n+1} = t_n + 2 - 2y/x$$

One final simplification may be made to remove the division operation (eliminating the fractional part and leaving the equation as pure integer math). Multiply through by x to get $xt_{n+1} = xt_n - 2y$ for $y_{n+1} = y_n$, and $xt_{n+1} = xt_n + 2y + 2x$ for $y_{n+1} = y_{n+1}$. If you always compute xt_n and xt_{n+1}, the next value is always found from the current value by either subtracting 2y (for positive or zero values), or adding $2x - 2y$ (for negative values). Don't forget that the initial t value, $t_1 = 1$, must also be multiplied by x: $xt_1 = x$. Also note that we already know the location of the first point and that x is positive, so we can find $xt_2 = x - 2y$.

We now have a complete algorithm for finding a line which starts from the left and goes right with a slope less than 1 (up on cartesian coordinates, and down the display):

Start with the two endpoints of a line, (x_a,y_a) and (x_b,y_b). Select the leftmost point (smallest x coordinate) as the starting point; we will assume (x_a,y_a) is the leftmost point.

Find $x = x_b - x_a$ and $y = y_b - y_a$. Use them to calculate the test value for the second point: $x - 2y$. Also calculate the two possible adjustments to the test value, $p = 2y$ and $n = 2x - 2y$.

Plot the first point, and repeat the next three steps until the last point has been plotted.

1. If the test value is zero or positive, subtract p and do not change the y coordinate. If it is negative, add n and increment the y coordinate by 1.
2. Increment the x coordinate by 1.
3. Plot the new (x,y).

Note that when working with actual endpoints, all initial values are integers. And since only addition and subtraction are involved, all results are integers also.

Now, we just need a method for the remaining three cases (up and down will refer to up and down the face of the display): starting from the left, moving mostly right and up; starting from the top moving mostly down and right; and starting from the top, moving mostly down and left.

While still moving mostly right, the constants based on the y axis will switch sign, and the y coordinate will be decremented rather than incremented. Thus p = -2y and n = 2x + 2y.

To move mostly down and right, the x and y terms should be swapped (in the original derivation). Thus, y would always be incremented, the x coordinate incremented when the test value is negative, p = 2x and n = 2y − 2x. To move mostly down and to the left, the sign of the x coordinate constants will change, giving p = -2x and n = 2y + 2x, and, of course, the x coordinate would be decremented for a positive test value.

The Ellipse Algorithm

The derivation for the elliptical algorithm is similar to that of the line algorithm. We can arbitrarily start with any point on the circumference of the ellipse, move one pixel in the x (or y) direction, and then decide whether to also move one pixel in the y (or x) direction. As with Bresenham's line algorithm, we can choose either the same y value or change the value by one, based on a comparison to the "true" value. Thus the algorithm is based on a series of additions and subtractions rather than evaluating square roots.

Start with the equation for an ellipse centered at 0,0:

$$y^2 = r_2{}^2 - r_2{}^2 x^2/r_1{}^2$$

Then let $e = r_2/r_1$:

$$y^2 = r_2{}^2 - e^2 x^2 \qquad \text{Eq. 1}$$

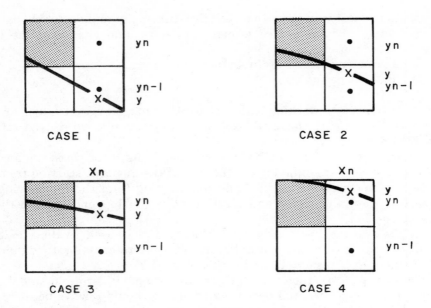

Figure 15-2 Four closest fit possibilities for an ellipse

Imagine starting near the top right center of the ellipse, moving to the right one pixel (to x_n), and choosing the next y (y_n). Note that x_n is known, and y_n will be close to a value which we will call y_n or $y_n - 1$ since y_n is probably not an integer. Note that we use $y_n - 1$ instead of $y_n + 1$ because we are moving down. Since each location must be represented by an integer, the new position may not be the true y value. We can express this as a difference (one for each of our test cases y_n and $y_n - 1$):

$$d_1 = y_n^2 - y^2$$
$$d_2 = y^2 - (y_n - 1)^2$$

We want to choose the value (y_n or $y_n - 1$) which is closer to the correct y: in other words the y associated with the smaller of the two d's. We can devise a test parameter, t, which chooses between the two on the basis of the sign (positive or negative). To do this:

$$t_n = d_1 - d_2$$
$$t_n = y_n^2 - 2y^2 + (y_n - 1)^2 \qquad \text{Eq. 2}$$

which gives four possibilities (shown graphically in Figure 15-2):

case	d_1	d_2	t_n	choose
1) $y_n > y$ and $y_n - 1 >= y$	+g	−s	+	$y_n - 1$

2) $y_n > y$ and $y_n - 1 < y$ +g   +s   + $y_n - 1$
3) $y_n > = y$ and $y_n - 1 < y$ +s   +g   − y_n
4) $y_n < = y$ and $y_n - 1 < y$ −s   +g   − y_n
g = greater absolute value, s = smaller absolute value.

Note that it would be impossible for $y_n < y$ while $y_n - 1 > 1$ since $y_n > y_n - 1$, so this case was not included in the possibilities.

Now substitute Eq. 1 into Eq. 2:

$$t_n =$$
$$y_n^2 - 2(r_2^2 - e^2 x_n^2) + (y_n - 1)^2 =$$
$$y_n^2 - 2r_2^2 + 2e^2 x_n^2 + y_n^2 - 2y_n + 1 =$$
$$2y_n^2 - 2r_2^2 + 2e^2 x_n^2 - 2y_n + 1$$

and find the next text point:

$$t_{n+1} = y_{n+1}^2 - 2r_2^2 + 2e^2(x_n + 1)^2 + (y_{n+1} - 1)^2$$
$$= 2y_{n+1}^2 - 2r_2^2 + 2e^2(x_n^2 + 2x_n + 1) - 2y_{n+1} + 1$$

expressed in terms of t_n:

$$t_{n+1} = t_n + 2y_{n+1}^2 - 2y_n^2 + 4e^2 x_n + 2e^2 + 2y_n - 2y_{n+1}$$
$$= t_n + 2y_{n+1}^2 - 2y_n^2 + 2y_n - 2y_{n+1} + 4e^2 x_n + 2e^2$$

Now, the equation for t_{n+1} can take either of two forms, depending on the value of y_{n+1}:

for $y_{n+1} = y_n$:
     $t_{n+1} = t_n + 4e^2 x_n + 2e^2$
for $y_{n+1} = y_n - 1$
     $t_{n+1} = t_n + 2[(y_n - 1)^2 - y_n^2] + 2[y_n - (y_n - 1)] + 4e^2 x_n + 2e^2$
     $t_{n+1} = t_n + 2[y_n^2 - 2y_n + 1 - y_n^2] + 2 + 4e^2 x_n + 2e^2$
     $t_{n+1} = t_n - 4y_n + 2 + 2 + 4e^2 x_n + 2e^2$
     $t_{n+1} = t_n - 4y_n + 4 + 4e^2 x_n + 2e^2$

The two forms of t_n given above are used to determine whether y remains the same or is decremented by one. Also, it is used to find the next t_n. The algorithm starts at coordinates to $(0, r_2)$, increments x, calculates each successive t_n from the two equations above, and decides whether or not to decrement y.

Set $x = 0$ and $y = r_2$ and find the initial value of t. By substituting 0 and r_2 for x and y, this can be simplified to $t_n = - 2r_2 + 1$. Because we want to use avoid division (remember that $e = r_2 / r_1$), all of the equations should be multiplied by r_1^2. Since t_n is relative (it depends on previous values), we will continue to use t_n even though it is really $t_n r_1^2$. This gives $t_n = - 2r_2 r_1^2 + r_1^2$. The t_{n+1} equations become

$4r_2{}^2x_n + 2r_2{}^2$, and $-4r_1{}^2y_n + 4r_1{}^2 + 4r_2{}^2x_n + 2r_2{}^2$. Note that there are two recurring parameters: $4r_2{}^2x_n + 2r_2{}^2$ (initially $2r_2{}^2$, and increased by $4r_2{}^2$ with each iteration), and $4r_1{}^2 - 4r_1{}^2y_n$ (initially $4r_1{}^2 - 4r_1{}^2y_n$, and increased by $4r_1{}^2$ each time y is decremented). Also note that these values apply to t_n, which describes the first point (which we already know). We must adjust to t_{n+1} before plotting the point.

Now use the following procedure until $x = (r_1{}^4 / (r_1{}^2 + r_2{}^2))^{1/2}$:

1. Plot (x,y).
2. If $t_n = 0$ add $4r_1{}^2 - 4r_1{}^2y_n$ to t_n and decrement y. Add $4r_1{}^2$ to $4r_1{}^2 - 4r_1{}^2y_n$ for the next usage.
3. Add $4r_2{}^2x_n + 2r_2{}^2$ to t_n and increment x. Add $4r_2{}^2$ to $4r_2{}^2x_n + 2r_2{}^2$ for the next iteration.

Note that by definition, these equations assume that the slope is no more than 45 degrees, since an increment of 1 in the x direction can be countered by nothing greater than a change of 1 in the y direction. Thus, the algorithm presented can only be used until the slope reaches 45 degrees. This is the point where $x = (r_1{}^4 / (r_1{}^2 + r_2{}^2))^{1/2}$. You can calculate this for yourself, if you wish, by taking the derivative of equation 1, setting $f'(y) = 1/2$, and solving the resulting equation for x.

Since the numbers often exceed 16-bit limits, the routine must use at least 32-bit arithmetic. In one case, I have expanded a temporary result to 48 bits. You could also use the larger integers provided on the 8087 or the 80386, to increase the execution speed. If you write a version for the 8087, be sure to use the stack for the iterative portions of the code.

Pixel plotting, ellipses, and lines form a solid foundation for most graphics applications. Of course, many other issues may be relevant to your applications, such as filling, three-dimensional drawing, rotation, spline curves, and scaling. With a solid understanding of hardware considerations, you should be able to write efficient routines for these functions. Many books are available which cover these topics in general terms — usually giving high level language algortihms. An excellent book full of such algorithms is *Computer Graphics* by Donald Hearn and M. Pauline Baker.

Bresenham's derivation may be applied to equations other than linear and elliptical equations. M.L.V. Pitteway gives a rigorous derivation for a generalized conic section (including rotations) in an article titled "Algorithm for Drawing Ellipses or Hyperbolae with a Digital Plotter", *Computer Journal*, Volume 10, Issue 3, pages 282-289. You may also find that you are regularly plotting another equation which would benefit from these techniques.

The appendices contain programs (including the ellipse and line algorithms) which have been optimized for particular functions. In some cases, such as the stand-alone plotting algorithm, the optimization assumes certain screen dimensions. You may find that mixing methods from various programs will increase the efficiency; if you will be plotting circles only in 640 x 350 mode, you may want to try using the stand-alone plot routine in the ellipse program. You should also look for additional ways to optimize (or improve) the programs.

Appendix

The program **FPLOT.ASM** draws a line of colored dots across row 10 of the display. The resulting screen is identical to the program under BIOS function 0 in Chapter 2. However, FPLOT skips the BIOS plot routine and writes directly to the adapter hardware. Note that the plot routine is hard coded for an 80-column screen — the sequence of shifts and adds to multiply by 80 is fast, but not very flexible. Furthermore, the shift and add sequence is slightly more efficient than a register MUL on the 8088, but on any other processor (including the 80286 and NEC V20), the MUL instruction is faster by about the same factor. The difference either way is almost insignificant, but it shows how a different approach may make a difference (and that the results may be hardware dependent).

Assembly Language Example:

```
ega        segment at 0a000h

ega        ends

data       segment public

           clr     db        16      ;color initially set to 16

data       ends

code       segment public
           assume CS:code

main       proc    far

start:     push    DS
           sub     AX,AX
           push    AX

           mov     AX,data
           mov     DS,AX
           assume  DS:data
```

```
            mov     AX,ega
            mov     ES,AX
            assume  ES:ega

            mov     AH,0        ;select function 0  set mode
            mov     AL,10h      ;select mode 10h
            int     10h         ;BIOS video call

            mov     CX,639      ;this will be the column

lp:         mov     AL,clr      ;set color
            dec     AX          ;subtract one from the color
            mov     clr,AL      ;store the new color
            jnz     skip        ;if the color is not 0
                                ; then continue to skip
            mov     clr,16      ;set the color back to 16

skip:       mov     DX,10       ;set the row to 10
            push    AX          ;preserve last color
            push    CX          ;preserve last column
            call    plot        ;plot the point
            pop     CX          ;restore last column
            pop     AX          ;restore last color
            loop    lp          ;decrement CX (next column)

            mov     AX,0ff08h   ;Bit Mask register, enable all bits
            mov     DX,3ceh     ;graphics 1 and 2 address register
            out     DX,AX       ;write to both graphics & bit mask
            mov     AX,0f02h    ;Map Mask register, enable all maps
            mov     DX,3c4h     ;Sequencer Address register
            out     DX,AX       ;write to both the Add. & Mask regs

            ret

main        endp

plot        proc    near

            push    AX          ;save the color for later
```

;the following section multiplies row # by 80 (640 / 8) 640
; bits/row/8 bits/byte = 80 bytes/row the shift and add sequence
; is faster than a MUL

```
            mov     BX,DX       ;put the row in BX
            push    CX          ;save column (restore in BX)
            and     CX,7        ;get bit offset (remainder of /8)
```

```
        mov     AH,80h
        shr     AH,CL       ;make Bit Mask
        mov     AL,8        ;index for Bit Mask register
        mov     DX,3ceh     ;Graphics 1 and 2 Address register
        out     DX,AX       ;write to both Graphics & Bit Mask
        mov     AX,BX       ;row ...
        shl     AX,1        ; * 2
        shl     AX,1        ; * 4
        add     AX,BX       ; * 5
        shl     AX,1        ; * 10
        shl     AX,1        ; * 20
        shl     AX,1        ; * 40
        shl     AX,1        ; * 80
                            ;now add the col # / 8
        pop     BX          ;column # (pushed as CX)
        shr     BX,1
        shr     BX,1
        shr     BX,1
        add     BX,AX

        mov     AL,ES:[BX];load the latch registers

        mov     DX,3c4h     ;Sequencer Address register
        mov     AX,0f02h    ;all planes, index 2 (Map Mask reg.)
        out     DX,AX       ;write to both the Add. & Mask regs

        mov     byte ptr ES:[BX],0  ;clear any current colors

        pop     AX          ;restore the color
        inc     DX          ;point to just the Map Mask
        out     DX,AL       ;set the color
        mov     byte ptr ES:[BX],0ffh         ;plot the point

        ret

plot    endp

code    ends

end     start
```

SMOOTH.ASM creates a virtual screen 104 characters wide and 73 lines long. The screen is filled with the letters of the alphabet with varying attributes. It then smoothly scrolls down and right from the upper, left corner in a stair-step manner. Upon reaching the right edge, the right scroll switches to a left scroll. The scrolling is done in alphanumeric mode; graphics mode scrolling is very similar (and a bit simpler). The process is described in Chapter 14.

Assembly Language Example:

```
clr_flg      equ      1
ecd_flg      equ      2
g64_flg      equ      4
vga_flg      equ      8
c_wide       equ      104        ;width of the virtual screen
lines        equ      (c_wide-80)*2+25
ATC_add      equ      3c0h    ;Attribute Controller address
lc_a         equ      'a'

word_out    macro
;;
;;most adapter/computer combinations accept a word OUT
;;instruction, however a few combinations balk at this. A good way
;;to handle this is with a macro for all OUT instructions. If someone
;;has a problem with your program, you can recompile it with byte out
;;routines simply by changing the macro to the commented section.
;;
             out      DX,AX
;;
;;           out      DX,AL
;;           xchg     AL,AH
;;           inc      DX
;;           out      DX,AL
;;           xchg     AL,AH
;;           dec      DX
;;
             endm

byte_out    macro
;;
             out      DX,AL
             xchg     AL,AH
             out      DX,AL
             xchg     AL,AH
;;
             endm
disp        macro
```

```
            local rt
;;This macro drops through only during a display interval
;;DX must be already set to 3c0h (used in DISPLAY and WAIT_D
;;macros)
;;
rt:         in      AL,DX    ;;test vertical retrace status bit
            test    AL,1000b ;;is it in a vertical retrace?
            jnz     rt       ;; yes, keep looking for non-retrace
                             ;;(display) interval

;;
            endm


display     macro
;;
            mov     DX,st_add ;;Input Status Register One
            disp
;;
            endm


retr        macro
            local n_rt

;;macro which drops through only during a vertical retrace
;;DX must be already set to 3c0h (used in RETRACE and WAIT_R
;;macros)
;;
n_rt:       in      AL,DX    ;;check for the beginning of the
                             ;;vertical retrace.
            test    AL,1000b ;;Is it in a vertical retrace?
            jz      n_rt     ;; no, try again.
;;
            endm


retrace     macro
;;
            mov     DX,st_add ;;Input Status Register One
            retr
;;
            endm

wait_r      macro
;;
;;This macro will drop through only at the beginning of a vertical
```

```
;;retrace it first waits for a display interval, and only then looks for a
;;retrace
;;
                display
                retr
;;
                endm

wait_d          macro
;;
                retrace
                disp
;;

                endm

fill_alpha      macro
                local keep,lp
;;
;; This macro fills the data area with the letters of the alphabet
;; and a cycle attribute bytes
;;
lp:             mov     [BX],AX
                add     AX,101h ;;next letter
                add     BX,2    ;;next memory address
                cmp     AH,14   ;;is the attribute now 14?
                jne     keep    ;; no, keep it
                mov     AH,18   ;;skip cyan on cyan
keep:           loop    lp
;;
                endm

data            segment public

                ltrs    db      c_wide*2+25*2 dup (?);letters A...Z...
                                                ;and attributes

;
;The area above will be filled by the program to save typing
;and will look like:
;
;               ltrs    db      'a.b.c.d.e.f.g.h.i.j.k.l.m.n.o.p.q.r.s.t.u.v.w.
;                       db      'x.y.z.'
;                       db      'a.b.c.d.e.f.g.h.i.j.k.l.m.n.o.p.q.r.s.t.u.v.w.
;                       db      'x.y.z.'
;                               etc.
;where "." represents an attribute byte. It is long enough to fill a full
;104 char line starting with any letter of the alphabet (offset 0-25).
```

```
            hdwre   db      ?
even
            strt_add label  byte
            strt_addw       dw      2 dup (0);adapter (internal)
                                            ;memory address
            CRT_add         dw      3b4h    ;CRTC port
            st_add  dw      ?               ;input status register
                                            ;one address
            al_seg  dw      0b000h          ;alpha mode segment
            ch_hi   dw      13              ;character height
                                            ;minus 1
            ch_wi   dw      8               ;character width
                                            ;minus 1
            al_mode db      7               ;alpha mode

data        ends

code        segment public
            assume  CS:code

main        proc    far

start:      push    DS
            sub     AX,AX
            push    AX

            mov     AX,data
            mov     DS,AX
            assume  DS:data

            mov     BX,offset ltrs      ;address of letters

; fill the character/attribute data area

            mov     CX,c_wide/26
lp:         push    CX
            mov     CX,26       ;all 26 letters of the alphabet
            mov     AL,lc_a     ;start with a lowercase 'a'
            mov     AH,1        ;start with attribute 1
                                ;(don't use black on black)
            fill_alpha
            pop     CX
            loop    lp

            mov     AL,lc_a     ;start with 'a' again
            mov     AH,1        ;add attribute 1
            mov     CX,25       ;but only go to 'y'
```

```
            fill_alpha

            mov      AX,1a00h ;read display combination
            int      10h         ;BIOS video call

            cmp      AL,1ah  ;the VGA (or Model 30) will return 1ah
            jne      not_vga

            cmp      BL,7    ;is it a monochrome VGA?
            je       yes_vga
            cmp      BL,8    ;is it a color VGA?
            je       yes_vga
            jmp      not_vga ;could check for EGA for completeness

yes_vga:    or       hdwre,vga_flg

not_vga:    mov      BL,10h  ;get EGA information
            mov      AH,12h  ;alternate functions
            int      10h     ;BIOS call


            cmp      BH,1    ;Is it a monochrome
            je       mono    ;yes, defaults already set for
                            ;monochrome, skip setup

            cmp      CL,1001b ;Check switch settings.
                             ; Is it an enhanced display?
            je       ecd
            cmp      CL,0011b ; in hi-res alpha mode
            je       ecd
;must be a normal color display (or ECD in emulation mode)
            mov      ch_hi,7
            jmp      cd

ecd:        or       hdwre,ecd_flg     ;set the ECD flag

;the following section is common between standard color and ECD

cd:         or       hdwre,clr_flg     ;set the color flag
            mov      ch_wi,7           ;character width is 8 for
                                      ;non-VGA, or VGA in 8 dot
                                      ;mode
            mov      al_seg,0b800h     ;alpha mode address for all
                                      ;color modes
            mov      al_mode,3         ;mode 3 for alpha mode
            mov      CRT_add,3d4h      ;CRT address is 3d4h for all
                                      ;color modes
```

```
            test      hdwre,vga_flg      ;VGA may be in 9 dot mode
            jz        only_8             ; if not VGA, don't to check

            mov       DX,3c4h            ;sequencer address register
            mov       AL,1     ;clocking mode index
            out       DX,AL
            inc       DX       ;point to clocking mode register
            in        AL,DX    ;if bit 1 = 1, the dot clock is 8
            test      AL,1
            jnz       only_8
            mov       ch_wi,8  ;character width is 9 for VGA in 9
                               ;dot mode
only_8:

mono:       test      hdwre,vga_flg    ;VGA may be 16 lines high
            jz        def_hi   ; if not VGA, use default height

            mov       ch_hi,15 ;store height-1 (16 pixels on VGA)

def_hi:     mov       AX,CRT_add
            add       AX,6     ;Status Address Register One is CRTC+6
            mov       st_add,AX
```

;START ALPHA MODE SCROLLING DEMONSTRATION

```
            xor       AH,AH    ;function call 0 — set mode
            mov       AL,al_mode          ;make sure alpha mode is set
            int       10h      ;BIOS video call

            mov       AX,al_seg          ;set ES:DI to the beginning
                                         ;of alpha memory
            mov       ES,AX
            assume    ES:nothing
            mov       DI,0

            cli                ;disable interrupts

            wait_r             ;wait for the vertical retrace
            mov       DX,CRT_add
            mov       AL,13h   ;offset register index
            mov       AH,c_wide/2         ;use the same virtual width
                                          ;for all alpha modes
            word_out
```

;we will leave the start address at 0 (upper, left corner)
;although you may want to use a different initial start address

```
;in your applications
;WRITE THE TEXT TO THE SCREEN THROUGH THE MOVE
;STRING INSTRUCTION

            mov      BX,offset ltrs        ;get the starting letter's
                                           ;address
            xchg     AH,AL    ;put word width in AL
            xor      AH,AH    ;0 out AH
            shl      AX,1     ;multiply by two to include
                             ;attribute bytes

            mov      CX,lines

n_line:     push     CX       ;save outer loop value
            mov      SI,BX    ;put starting letter in SI
            mov      CX,AX    ;count for entire line width
            rep      movsw    ;move a full virtual display line into
                             ;display mem
            add      BX,2     ;start with the next letter of the alphabet
            cmp      BX,offset ltrs+26*2 ;is it past z?
            jne      n_ltr    ;no, start next line with next letter
            sub      BX,52    ;yes, start with 'a' again
n_ltr:      pop      CX       ;restore outer loop value
            loop     n_line   ;do next line

            sti               ;re-enable interrupts

;START SMOOTH SCROLLING THROUGH THE DISPLAY (DOWN
;ONE CHAR AND RIGHT ONE CHAR)

            mov      CX,-80   ;CX contains width of screen as a
                             ;negative number
            add      CX,c_wide         ;add virtual screen width to
                                       ;get number of characters
                                       ;between the right edge of
                                       ;actual and virtual screen
            push     CX       ;save this value for use in second section

again:      call     down_c

            call     right_c
            loop     again
;START MOVING DOWN ONE CHAR AND LEFT ONE CHAR

            pop      CX

again2:     call     down_c
```

```
          call      left_c
          loop      again2

          xor       AH,AH    ;function call 0 — set mode
          mov       AL,al_mode         ;end program with alpha
                                       ;mode reset
          int       10h      ;BIOS video call

          ret

main      endp

right_c   proc      near
```

; Move the display area one character to the right in text mode

```
          push      AX
          push      BX
          push      CX
          push      DX

          mov       CX,ch_wi
          mov       BX,0033h;index of horizontal pel panning
                                       ;(start at 0 for 9 bit)
                                       ;bit 5 is set (palette registers remain
                                       ;unmodified)
          cmp       ch_wi,8  ;was it a 9 bit character width
                             ; (ch_wi = width - 1)
          je        is_9     ; yes, skip next step
          inc       BH       ; no, start at 1 for 8 bit
          cli                ;do not allow interrupts (to prevent
                             ;register changes)
is_9:     wait_r             ;wait for vertical retrace (modifies
                             ;AX/DX)
                             ;also provides required resetting of 3c0h
          mov       DX,ATC_add         ;attribute register
          mov       AX,BX
          byte_out           ;most cards will accept OUT DX,AX to
                             ;3c0h, although it is undocumented
          inc       BH       ;next step of horizontal scroll
          loop      is_9     ;loop for one full character width

          cmp       ch_wi,8  ;was it a 9 bit character width
                             ;(ch_wi = width - 1)
          je        is_9_2   ; yes, skip next step
          mov       BH,0     ; no, start at 0 for 8 bit
is_9_2:   display            ;Start address must be set during display interval
```

```
                              ;to take effect  at the beginning next vertical
                                     ; retrace

              inc      strt_addw            ;point to the next character
                                            ;for display start address
              mov      DX,CRT_add
              mov      AL,0ch   ;index of start address high
              mov      AH,strt_add[1]       ;get the most significant byte
              word_out
              inc      AX       ;index of start address low
              mov      AH,strt_add          ;get the least significant byte
              word_out

              retrace  ;the above code is during the display interval
                       ; no need to check again with the WAIT_R macro
              mov      DX,ATC_add
              mov      AX,BX
              byte_out

              sti

              pop      DX
              pop      CX
              pop      BX
              pop      AX

              ret

right_c       endp

left_c        proc     near

; Move the display area one character to the right in text mode

              push     AX
              push     BX
              push     CX
              push     DX

              cli      ;do not allow interrupts
                       ;(to prevent register changes)
              display  ;Start address must be set during
                       ;display interval to take effect
                       ;at the beginning next vertical retrace
              dec      strt_addw            ;point to the next character
                                            ;for display start address
              mov      DX,CRT_add
```

```
            mov     AL,0ch   ;index of start address high
            mov     AH,strt_add[1]     ;get the most significant byte
            word_out
            inc     AX       ;index of start address low
            mov     AH,strt_add        ;get the least significant byte

            word_out

            mov     CX,ch_wi
            inc     CX
            mov     BX,0733h ;index of horizontal pel
                             ;panning (start at 7th pixel)
                             ;bit 5 is set (palette registers remain
                             ;unmodified)

lp_lft:     wait_r           ;wait for vertical retrace
                             ;(modifies AX/DX) also provides
                             ;required resetting of 3c0h
            mov     DX,ATC_add         ;attribute register
            mov     AX,BX
            byte_out         ;most cards will accept OUT DX,AX
                             ;to 3c0h, although undocumented
            dec     BH       ;next step of horizontal scroll
            loop    lp_lft   ;loop for the remaining bits
                             ;(unless 9 bit width)

            cmp     ch_wi,8  ;was it a 9 bit character width
                             ; (ch_wi = width - 1)
            jne     not_9    ; yes, skip next step
            mov     BH,0     ; no, start at 0 for 8 bit
            wait_r
            mov     DX,ATC_add
            mov     AX,0833h ;set the Pel Pan register to 8 for
                             ;9 bit width
            byte_out

not_9:      sti

            pop     DX
            pop     CX
            pop     BX
            pop     AX

            ret
left_c      endp

down_c      proc    near
```

; Move the display area one character to the right in text mode

```
            push    AX
            push    BX
            push    CX
            push    DX

            mov     CX,ch_hi
            mov     BX,0108h    ;index of preset row scan
                                ;(start at 1)
            cli                 ;do not allow interrupts (to prevent
                                ;register changes)
lp_d:       wait_r              ;wait for retrace interval
                                ;(modifies AX/DX)

            mov     DX,CRT_add          ;CRTC register address
            mov     AX,BX
            word_out
            inc     BH          ;next step of vertical scroll
            loop    lp_d        ;loop for one full character height

            mov     BX,c_wide           ;width of virtual screen
            add     BX,strt_addw        ;BX points to the next line
            mov     strt_addw,BX        ;save the new start address

            wait_d              ;wait for display interval to change
                                ;start address

            mov     DX,CRT_add
            mov     AL,0dh      ;index of start address high
            mov     AH,BL       ;get the least significant byte
            word_out
            dec     AX          ;index of start address low
            mov     AH,BH       ;get the most significant byte
            word_out

            retrace             ;wait until retrace to modify preset
                                ;row scan
            mov     DX,CRT_add
            mov     AX,8        ;set preset row scan to 0
            word_out
            wait_d              ;prevents next call from occurring in
                                ;the same interval
            sti

            pop     DX
            pop     CX
```

```
            pop     BX
            pop     AX

            ret

down_c      endp

down_p      proc    near

; Move the display area one character to the right in text mode

            push    AX
            push    BX
            push    CX
            push    DX

            cli

            mov     BX,c_wide        ;width of virtual screen
            add     BX,strt_addw     ;BX points to the next line
            mov     strt_addw,BX     ;save the new start address

            wait_d                   ;wait for display interval to change
                                     ;start address

            mov     DX,CRT_add
            mov     AL,0dh  ;index of start address high
            mov     AH,BL   ;get the least significant byte
            word_out
            dec     AX      ;index of start address low
            mov     AH,BH   ;get the most significant byte
            word_out

            sti

            pop     DX
            pop     CX
            pop     BX
            pop     AX
            ret

down_p      endp

code        ends

end         start
```

ELLIPSE.ASM uses integer techniques to plot an ellipse. Note the use of macros to define the function. The macro E_PROC jumps around the ellipse routine, and then redefines itself as a NEAR call to the routine. Note that the first usage defines the parameter passing — the use of parameters after ELLIPSE is not strictly necessary after the first call, since all variables will be referenced by the first names given. The algorithm is derived in Chapter 15.

Assembly Language Example:

```
PAGE ,132

;This program does not check the range. A range checking
;procedure within the plotting routine is generally a good
;idea unless the program itself will limit the size and
;placement of the ellipses. You might also want to make
;modifications to draw arcs (perhaps by modifying placing
;variable limits on the x and y coordinates of the plot routine).
;Also note that the algorithm will fail if the dependent variable
;(y) becomes zero. If your application will not constrain the
;radii, the program should be modified to stop adjusting y if
;it becomes 0.

;I assumed neither radius would exceed 640 pixels — this should
;be large enough for most practical applications.

ep_type='mv'            ;Ellipse parameters in memory
                        ; variables.
                        ; Use 'rg' for parameters in
                        ; registers
r_l       equ   00000001b         ;mask which designates the
                                  ; right
                        ; and left end arcs are being
                        ; plotted (stored in "portion")
t_b       equ   11111110b         ;mask which designates the
                                  ; top and
                        ; bottom arcs are being plotted
                        ; (stored in "portion").

pixpb     equ   3       ;pixels per byte (in shifts)
                        ; 2^3 = 8 pixels
b_mask    equ   10000000b         ;bit mask (will be rotated)


word_out  macro

          out    DX,AX
```

```
            endm

; THE FOLLOWING MACROS ARE FOR THE ELLIPSE
; PROCEDURES

e_d         macro

data        segment public

            even                            ;align on even address

            t_e_lo  dw      ?

            t_e_hi  dw      ?
            r1_lo   dw      ?
            r1_hi   dw      ?
            r2_lo   dw      ?
            r2_hi   dw      ?
            y_p_lo  dw      ?
            y_p_hi  dw      ?

            max_x   dw      ?

            c_x     dw      ?
            c_y     dw      ?

            x       dw      ?
            y       dw      ?

            portion db      ?

            bprow   dw      80      ;bytes/row (640 bits / 8)
            ega_mem         dw      0a000h

data        ends

            endm


e_proc      macro   xl,yl,r1l,y2l

            jmp     skip_proc
ellip       proc    near
```

; COMPUTE INITIAL VALUES
; These values are calculated only twice per ellipse to avoid
; repeating time intensive calculations. Optimization of these

```
; routines is not nearly as important as those within the
; plotting loop. Note the calculation of the maximum x value.
; While it is rather long, the simple compare after each loop
; will usually be much faster than multiplying x and y by the
; appropriate factors, and then comparing. You could also
; calculate both sets of arcs simultaneously until the sections
; meet, but many more (slow) memory accesses would be required
; to store all of the additional variables.

;                 AX contains x
;                 BX contains r2
;                 CX contains r1


          mov     SI,AX    ;save x in SI

          mov     AX,BX
          mul     BX       ;AX+DX = r2^2
          mov     BP,DX
          mov     BX,AX    ;BX+BP = r2^2
          mov     r2_lo,AX
          mov     r2_hi,DX;also store in memory

          mov     AX,CX
          mul     CX       ;AX+DX = r1^2
          mov     DI,DX
          mov     CX,AX    ;CX+DI = r1^2
          mov     r1_lo,AX
          mov     r1_hi,DX;also store in memory

;CX = LSW of r1^2
;DI = MSW of r1^2
;BX = LSW of r2^2
;BP = MSW of r2^2
;SI = x

;Calculate the maximum x (stopping point)
; [r1^4/(r2^2+r1^2)]^-1/2
; because r1^4 could exceed 32 bits (640^4), the following
; section uses 48 bit arithmetic for some operations
; this code assumes DX+AX and CX+DI contain r1^2
; and uses this technique:
;       hw lw
;       x hw lw
;
;     --------
;     lw  x lw             low word squared
;     lw x hw   (x 2^16)
```

```
;     lw x hw    (x 2^16)    2 * low word * high word
;   + hw x hw    (x 2^32)    high word squared
;
; Note that the values are always positive

            push    BX      ;save the registers
            push    CX
            push    DI
            push    BP
            push    SI

            mul     AX      ;low word squared
            mov     BP,AX   ;save in BP — low word is complete
            mov     BX,DX   ;save overflow in BX


            mov     AX,DI   ;get high word
            mul     CX      ;low word * high word
            shl     AX,1
            rcl     DX,1    ;2 * low word * high word
            add     BX,AX   ;middle word is now complete
            mov     CX,DX   ;save overflow in CX

            mov     AX,DI   ;get high word
            mul     AX      ;high word squared
            add     CX,AX   ;high word is now complete
                            ;DX is fourth word (assumed 0)

            mov     AX,BP   ;Least Significant Word in AX
                            ;Middle Significant Word in BX
                            ;Most Significant Word in CX
```

;now compute r2^2 + r1^2

```
            mov     DX,r2_lo ;put r2^2 in DI+DX
            mov     DI,r2_hi
            add     DX,r1_lo ;r2^2 + r1^2 (low word)
            adc     DI,r1_hi ;r2^2 + r1^2 (high word)
```

;now divide CX+BX+AX by DI+DX i.e. r1^4/(r1^2+r2^2)
; the 80x87 does this by subtracting the denominator until the
; numerator is less than the denominator. The count is the
; result, and the "numerator" is the remainder.

```
            mov     BP,0    ;set the count to 0
            mov     SI,0    ;count overflow set to 0
```

```
div_loop:
            cmp     CX,0        ;is the MSW 0?
            jne     c_div       ; no, continue the division
            cmp     BX,DI       ;is the num. MidSW > den. MSW?
            ja      c_div       ; yes, continue the division
            cmp     AX,DX       ;is the num. LSW >= den. LSW?
            jae     c_div       ; yes, continue the division
            jmp     div_done    ;the division operation is complete

c_div:      inc     BP          ;add one to the loop
            jnz     no_of       ;was there overflow?
            inc     SI          ; yes, increment the overflow
no_of:      sub     AX,DX       ;subtract the LSW's
            sbb     BX,DI       ;subtract the MidSW's
            sbb     CX,0        ;subtract MSW's (den. always 0)
            jmp     div_loop


div_done:
            shl     AX,1        ;multiply remainder by 2
            rcl     BX,1        ; assume CX=0 (highest realistic
                               ; value is 640^2)
            cmp     DI,BX       ;is the den. MSW > rem. MSW?
            ja      no_up       ; no, do not round result up
            cmp     DX,AX       ;is the den. LSW > rem. LSW?
            ja      no_up       ; no, do not round up

            inc     BP          ;the rem. >= 1/2*den., round up
            jnz     no_up       ;was there overflow?
            inc     SI          ; yes, increment the overflow

no_up:
;Now take the square root of the result. This is done by
; comparing the result to the squares of integers until the
; closest match is found. We will use a binary search between
; 0 and 1024 (which includes 640, the maximum radius)

            sub     BX,BX       ;starting value - 1 (=0)
            cmp     DX,0        ;check for 0
            jne     rt_strt     ; not 0, continue
            cmp     SI,0
            jne     rt_strt     ; still not 0 continue
            jmp     rt_done     ;must be 0, don't look for root

rt_strt:    mov     BX,512      ;starting test value
            mov     CX,512      ;change from test
rt_lp:      shr     CX,1        ;change / 2
```

```
            mov     AX,BX

            mul     AX          ;square of test value
            cmp     DX,SI       ;compare MSW's
            jg      t_lg        ; test is larger
            jl      t_sm        ; test is smaller
            cmp     AX,BP       ;can't tell — compare LSW's
            jb      t_sm        ; test is smaller
            jmp     t_lg        ;if test is larger (or equal)

t_sm:       add     AX,BX       ;add BX and check for sign change
            adc     DX,0
            cmp     SI,DX       ;i.e. is [t^2 <] x^2 <= t^2+t?
            ja      t_sm2       ;no, test is too small (x large)
            cmp     BP,AX       ; okay so far, check low word
            ja      t_sm2       ; test is still too small
            jmp     rt_done     ;we're as close as we're going
                                ;to get


t_sm2:      add     BX,CX       ;still too small, add change
            jmp     rt_lp       ; and continue search

t_lg:       sub     AX,BX       ;SUB BX and check for sign change
            sbb     DX,0
            cmp     DX,SI       ;i.e. is t^2-t < x^2 [<= t^2]
            ja      t_lg2       ; no, test is too large
            cmp     AX,BP       ; okay, so far, check low word
            ja      t_lg2       ; test is still too large

            jmp     rt_done     ;we're as close as we're going
                                ; to get
t_lg2:      sub     BX,CX       ;still to large, subract change
            jmp     rt_lp       ; and continue search

rt_done:    inc     BX          ;make sure it closes
            mov     max_x,BX

            pop     SI
            pop     BP
            pop     DI
            pop     CX
            pop     BX
```

;Calculate the initial test value (t_e = -2*r1^2*y+r1^2)

```
            push    BX          ;save r2^2
```

```
        push    BP

        mov     AX,CX   ;LSW of r1^2
        mul     y       ;y*r1^2 low word (two word result)
        mov     BX,AX   ;store in BX
        mov     BP,DX   ;store temp in BP
        mov     AX,DI   ;MSW of r1^2
        mul     y       ;y*r1^2 high word (DX will be 0
                        ; since 640^3 is a practical limit)
        add     BP,AX   ;add to overflow from previous MUL
                        ; [using the distributive property
                        ; y*(a+b) = y*a + y*b]
                        ; BP+BX contains y*r1^2

        neg     BX      ;-y*r1^2 (make 2's comp low word)
        not     BP      ;-y*r1^2 (make 2's comp high word)
        shl     BX,1    ;BX = 2*BX (low word)
        rcl     BP,1    ;BP = 2*BP (high word
                        ; plus high bit of low word)
                        ;BX+BP now contains -2*y*r1^2)


        add     CX,BX   ;DI+CX = -2*y*r1^2 + r1^2
        adc     DI,BP

        mov     t_e_lo,CX           ;store the LSW of t_e
        mov     t_e_hi,DI           ;store MSW of t_e
```

;calculate recurring parameters 4*r1^2*(-y+1), and 4*r^2*x+2*r^2
; requiring 4*r1^2, 4*r^2, and the initial values
; 4*r1^2*(-y_i+1)=-4*r1^2*(y_i-1) and 2*r2^2

```
        shl     r1_lo,1
        rcl     r1_hi,1
        shl     r1_lo,1
        rcl     r1_hi,1  ;r1_lo=4*r1^2
        mov     BX,y     ;put y_i in BX
        dec     BX       ;y_i-1
        mov     AX,r1_lo
        mul     BX       ;low word of 4*r1^2*(y_i-1)
        mov     BP,DX    ;temp. store the overflow in BP

        neg     AX       ;make 2's complement of low byte
                         ; i.e. AX=-4*r1^2*(y_i-1)

        mov     y_p_lo,AX           ;store the low word
        mov     AX,r1_hi
```

```
        mul      BX        ;high word of 2*r1^2*(2*y_i-1)
        add      AX,BP     ;add in the overflow

        not      AX        ;make 2's complement of high byte
        mov      y_p_hi,AX           ;save it for later use

        pop      BP        ;restore r2^2
        pop      BX

        shl      BX,1      ;2*r2^2
        rcl      BP,1

        push     BX        ;save temporarily
        push     BP        ;save temporarily

        shl      BX,1      ;4*r2^2
        rcl      BP,1
        mov      r2_lo,BX  ;save 4*r2^2
        mov      r2_hi,BP

        mov      CX,BX     ;change in x based term stored in
        mov      DI,BP     ;DI+CX=4*r2^2 (used each iteration)


        pop      BP        ;restore 2*r2^2 (initial x term)
        pop      BX        ;BP+BX=2*r2^2 (used each iteration)

        mov      DX,t_e_hi            ;put the test value in DX+AX
        mov      AX,t_e_lo

        ;initial x still in SI

retest:

; Plot the points

        push     AX
        push     BX
        push     CX
        push     DX
        push     DI
        push     SI
        push     BP

        mov      DI,y

old_type = ep_type
```

```
                    ep_type = 'rg'

            test        portion,r_l
            jz          no_xchg

            xchg        SI,DI

no_xchg:    mov         AL,color

            mov         CX,c_x
            add         CX,SI     ;column c_x+x
            mov         DX,c_y
            add         DX,DI     ;row c_y+y
            plot

            sub         CX,SI
            sub         CX,SI     ;column c_x-x (row c_y+y)
            plot

            sub         DX,DI
            sub         DX,DI     ;row c_y-y (column c_x-x)
            plot

            add         CX,SI

            add         CX,SI
            plot

                    ep_type = old_type

            pop         BP
            pop         SI
            pop         DI
            pop         DX
            pop         CX
            pop         BX
            pop         AX

            cmp         SI,max_x              ;have we done the last x?
            jne         e_cont    ; no, continue with next point
            jmp         e_done    ; yes, finish the procdure

e_cont:

; next test value

            cmp         DX,0      ;if the test value >= 0,
```

```
                                    ; add the y based term to the test
                                    ; value, then reduce y and change
                                    ; the y based term.
                                    ; Note that only high byte
                                    ; determines sign
            jl          less1       ;the value was < 0 so skip this

;add the y based term, 4*(r1^2 - y*r1^2)

            push        BX          ;save the x based term
            push        BP

            mov         BX,y_p_lo                   ;put the y term in BP+BX
            mov         BP,y_p_hi
            add         AX,BX       ;add the y term
            adc         DX,BP       ;to the test value

            dec         y           ;y=y-1

            add         BX,r1_lo    ;adjust the y based term
            adc         BP,r1_hi    ; to new 4*(r1^2 - r1^2*y)
                                    ; by adding 4*r1^2 (y decreased 1)

            mov         y_p_lo,BX
            mov         y_p_hi,BP                   ;save the new value

            pop         BP          ;restore x based term
            pop         BX

less1:      add         AX,BX       ;calculate the new test value
            adc         DX,BP       ; t_e = t_e + 4*x*r2^2 + 2*r2^2
                                    ;  (and maybe + 4*(r1^2 - y*r1^2))

            inc         SI          ;increment x

            add         BX,CX       ;adjust the x based term
            adc         BP,DI       ; by adding 4*r2^2 (x increased 1)

            jmp         retest

e_done:
            ret

ellip       endp

skip_proc:
```

```
            endm

e_call      macro    a,b,c,d

            push     AX
            push     BX
            push     CX
            push     DX

            mov      AX,a
            mov      c_x,AX
            mov      AX,b
            mov      c_y,AX
            mov      AX,0
            mov      x,0
            mov      BX,d
            mov      y,BX
            mov      CX,c
            call     ellip

            pop      DX
            pop      CX
            pop      BX
            pop      DX

            endm

ellipse     macro    xl,yl,r1l,r2l

            e_d                      ;;define the ellipse data area if this is
                                     ;;the first time
                                     ;; through the macro
            e_proc                   ;;define the ellipse procedure if this is
                                     ;; the first time through the macro
            set_mode
            and      portion,t_b
            e_call   xl,yl,r1l,r2l
            or       portion,r_l
            e_call   xl,yl,r2l,r1l
            rst_mode

            ellipse  macro

            set_mode
            and      portion,t_b
            e_call   xl,yl,r1l,r2l    ;;redefine ellipse as
                                     ;; only the call
```

```
                or          portion,r_l
                e_call      xl,yl,r2l,rll
                rst_mode

                        endm

                endm

rst_mode    macro
```

;;This macro restores the EGA write mode to the default (0)

```
                mov     DX,3ceh ;Address of the Graphics 1 and 2 register
                mov     AL,8    ;Index 8 (Bit map mask)
                mov     AH,0ffh ;restore bit mask to enable all
                                ; pixels in byte
                word_out

                mov     DX,3ceh ;graphics 1 and 2 address register
                mov     AL,5    ;set write mode
                mov     AH,0    ;mode 0 (BIOS default)
                word_out

                endm

set_mode    macro
```

;;This macro define defines the EGA write mode, sets the memory
;; address, and other overhead needed only once per call for
;; non-BIOS operation

```
                mov     DX,3ceh ;graphics 1 and 2 address register
                mov     AL,5    ;set write mode
                mov     AH,2    ;mode 2 (color n to masked bits)
                word_out

                endm


plot        macro
```

;Assumes page is 0, but similar to INT 10 in other respects:
;AL = color
;CX = column
;DX = row

```
                push    BX
```

```
        push    CX
        push    DX
        push    AX          ;done last for use near end

        push    DX

        mov     AX,CX       ;put the column number in AX
        push    CX          ;save the column number
        mov     CL,16-pixpb         ;find AX mod pixels per
                                    ; byte through shifts
        shl     AX,CL
        shr     AX,CL
        mov     CL,AL
        mov     AL,b_mask           ;create a bit mask by
        shr     AL,CL       ;rotate the bit mask into place
        pop     CX          ;restore CX

        mov     AH,AL       ;put the bit mask in AH
        mov     AL,8        ;bit mask register index
        mov     DX,3ceh     ;bit mask register
        word_out

        pop     DX

        mov     AX,DX               ;put the row in AX
        mov     BX,bprow            ;get bytes per row

        mul     BX                  ;multiply by bytes/row
        mov     BX,CX               ;put column number in BX
        mov     CL,pixpb
        shr     BX,CL               ;divide by pixels / byte
        add     BX,AX               ;byte offset in memory

        mov     AX,ega_mem
        mov     ES,AX
        mov     AL,ES:[BX]          ;load the latch registers
        pop     AX                  ;restore the color number
        mov     ES:[BX],AL          ;write color to memory

        pop     DX
        pop     CX
        pop     BX

        endm


plot2   macro   c,x,y
```

```
; Change this to PLOT (and PLOT to PLOT2) to see how much BIOS
; calls slow this program.

                push    AX

                mov     AH,0ch
                mov     BH,0
                int     10h

                pop     AX

                endm

; END OF MACROS — THE FOLLOWING CODE
; DEMONSTRATES THE USE OF THE
; ELLIPSE MACROS

dgroup      group   data

data        segment public

                r1      dw      100
                r2      dw      150
                cntr_x  dw      320
                cntr_y  dw      170

                color   db      5

                o_mode  db      ?
                o_curs  dw      ?

data        ends

code        segment public
            assume  cs:code

main        proc    far

start:      push    DS
            sub     AX,AX
            push    AX

            mov     AX,dgroup
            mov     DS,AX
            assume  DS:dgroup

            mov     AH,0fh  ;get current mode information
```

```
            int      10h
            mov      o_mode,AL          ;save the current mode

            mov      AH,3     ;get the cursor attributes
            int      10h
            mov      o_curs,CX          ;save the cursor type

            mov      AX,10h   ;set mode to hi-res graphics
            int      10h

            ellipse  cntr_x,cntr_y,r1,r2
            mov      r1,100
            mov      r2,100
            ellipse  cntr_x,cntr_y,r1,r2

            mov      AX,1000
bmrk:

            mov      color,al
            and      color,1111b
            push     AX
            mov      r1,50
            mov      r2,50
            ellipse  cntr_x,cntr_y,r1,r2

            pop      AX
            dec      AX

            jz       go_on
            jmp      bmrk
go_on:
            mov      AH,0     ;return mode to original value
            mov      AL,o_mode
            int      10h

            mov      AH,1     ;set cursor type
            mov      CX,o_curs            ;restore the cursor type
            int      10h

            ret

main        endp

code        ends

end         start
```

LINE.ASM uses integer techniques to plot a line. Note the use of macros to define the function. The macro L_PROC jumps around the line routine, and then redefines itself as a NEAR call to the routine. Note that the first usage defines the parameter passing — the use of parameters after LINE is not strictly necessary after the first call, since all variables will be referenced by the first names given. The algorithm is derived in Chapter 15.

Assembly Language Example:

PAGE ,132

```
;This program does not check the range. A range-checking
;procedure within the plotting routine is generally a good
;idea unless the program itself will limit the size and
;placement of the lines.

ln_type='mv'                     ;Line parameters in memory
                                 ; variables.
                                 ; Use 'rg' for parameters in
                                 ; registers

pixpb       equ     3            ;pixels per byte (in shifts)
                                 ; 2^3 = 8 pixels
b_mask      equ     10000000b            ;bit mask (will be rotated)

swap        equ     1            ;flag to swap x and y coordinates
neg_dx      equ     2            ;sign flag for delta x
neg_dy      equ     4            ;sign flag for delta y


word_out    macro

            out     DX,AX

            endm

; THE FOLLOWING MACROS ARE FOR THE LINE PROCEDURES

l_d         macro

data        segment public

            even                         ;align on even address

            bprow   dw      80           ;bytes/row (640 bits / 8)
            ega_mem         dw      0a000h
```

```
data          ends

              endm

;The following macro is the actual line algorithm. LABEL is
;the starting address, MAJ_DIR the major direction of travel
;("x" or "y"), and MIN_DIR the minor direction ("+" or "-").

;within the comments, X is the major direction and Y minor.

line_a        macro   label, maj_dir, min_dir
              local l_cont, grtr
label:
;; Plot the points

              push    AX

              old_type = ln_type
              ln_type = 'rg'

ifidn         <maj_dir>,<y>
              xchg    CX,DX
endif

              mov     AL,color
              plot

ifidn         <maj_dir>,<y>
              xchg    CX,DX
endif

              ln_type = old_type

              pop     AX

              cmp     CX,BX   ;;have we done the last y?
              jne     l_cont  ;; no, continue with next point
              jmp     l_done  ;; yes, finish the procedure

l_cont:

;; next test value

              cmp     AX,0
              jg      grtr    ;;the value was > 0, goto grtr
                              ;;test <= 0
              add     AX,DI   ;;test = test + 2*dx
```

```
ifidn       <min_dir>,<+>
            inc     DX          ;;y=y+1
else
            dec     DX          ;;y=y-1
endif

grtr:       sub     AX,SI       ;;test = test - 2*dy [+ 2*dx]

            inc     CX          ;;x=x+1
            jmp     label

            endm

l_proc      macro   xl,yl,r1l,y2l

            jmp     skip_proc
line_p      proc    near
```

; COMPUTE INITIAL VALUES

```
;           AX contains x_n
;           BX contains y_n
;           CX contains x_0
;           DX contains y_0
;           BP used for subroutine flags

            sub     BP,BP       ;clear all "flags"

            mov     DI,AX       ;put last x in DI
            sub     DI,CX       ;DI = delta x
                                ;SUB flags = CMP flags
            jae     p_dx        ;DI>=CX, delta x is positive

            neg     DI          ;we need a positive value
            or      BP,neg_dx           ; but we need the sign later

p_dx:       mov     SI,BX       ;put last y in DI
            sub     SI,DX       ;DX = delta y
            jae     p_dy        ;SI>=DX, delta x is positive

            neg     SI          ;we need a positive value
            or      BP,neg_dy           ; but we need the sign later

p_dy:       cmp     DI,SI       ;which is larger, dx or dy?
            jae     g_dx        ; delta x is larger (or equal)
```

;delta y is larger, so we must swap x and y values for the

;algorithm (and swap again when plotted).

```
        xchg    AX,BX    ;swap the x and y values
        xchg    CX,DX
        xchg    DI,SI
```

;swap the "flags"

```
        test    BP,neg_dx
        jz      no_dx
        or      BP,swap             ;use swap flag as temp
no_dx:  and     BP,not neg_dx       ;clear neg_dx
        test    BP,neg_dy                   ;was neg_dy set?
        jz      no_dy               ; no, skip next step
        or      BP,neg_dx                   ; yes, set neg_dx
no_dy:  and     BP,not neg_dy       ;clear neg_dy
        test    BP,swap             ;was neg_dx set?
        jz      no_tmp              ; no, skip next step
        or      BP,neg_dy                   ; yes, set neg_dy
no_tmp:
        or      BP,swap ;make sure swap is set

g_dx:   test    BP,neg_dx           ;check primary direction
        jz      r2l         ; (must be right to left)

                            ; it's right to left ...
        xchg    AX,CX       ; switch first and last x's
        xchg    BX,DX       ; switch first and last y's
        xor     BP,neg_dy           ; change the sign of delta y
                            ; algorithm assumes delta x>0.

r2l:    mov     BX,AX   ;put the last (max.) x in BX
;Calculate the initial test value (AX = delta x - 2 * delta y)

        mov     AX,DI   ;put delta x in AX
        shl     SI,1    ;SI = 2 * delta y
        sub     AX,SI   ;AX = delta x - 2 * delta y
```

;Calculate the recurring parameters 2 * dy (already done)
; and 2 * dx
```
        shl     DI,1    ;DI = 2 * delta x
```

;AX = test value
;BX = maximum x coordinate
;CX = current x coordinate
;DX = current y coordinate

```
;SI = 2 * delta y
;DI = 2 * delta x
;BP = swap and direction flags

;at this point, the four separate cases will be determined and
;run as different routine. These can easily be combined into
;a single routine, although performance will suffer slightly

                test      BP,swap

                jz        no_swp
                jmp       swap_p
no_swp:         test      BP,neg_dy
                jnz       retest2

                line_a    retest, x, +
                line_a    retest2, x, -

swap_p:         test      BP,neg_dy
                jnz       retest4

                line_a    retest3, y, +
                line_a    retest4, y, -

l_done:
                ret

line_p          endp

skip_proc:

                endm


line            macro     x1,y1,xn,yn

                l_d                     ;;define the line data area if this is the
                                        ;;first time through the macro
                l_proc                  ;;define the line procedure if this is the
                                        ;;first time through the macro
                set_mode
                push      AX
                push      BX
                push      CX
                push      DX

                mov       AX,xn
```

```
        mov     BX,yn
        mov     CX,x1
        mov     DX,y1

        call    line_p

        pop     DX
        pop     CX
        pop     BX
        pop     AX
        rst_mode


line    macro

        set_mode
        push    AX
        push    BX
        push    CX
        push    DX

        mov     AX,xn
        mov     BX,yn
        mov     CX,x1
        mov     DX,y1

        call    line_p

        pop     DX
        pop     CX
        pop     BX
        pop     AX
        rst_mode

        endm

    endm

rst_mode    macro

;;This macro restores the EGA write mode to the default (0)

        mov     DX,3ceh ;Address of the Graphics 1 and 2 register
        mov     AL,8    ;Index 8 (Bit map mask)
        mov     AH,0ffh ;restore bit mask to enable all
                        ; pixels in byte
        word_out
```

```
            mov     DX,3ceh ;graphics 1 and 2 address register
            mov     AL,5    ;set write mode
            mov     AH,0    ;mode 0 (BIOS default)
            word_out

            endm

set_mode    macro

;;This macro define defines the EGA write mode, sets the memory

;; address, and other overhead needed only once per call for
;; non-BIOS operation

            mov     DX,3ceh ;graphics 1 and 2 address register
            mov     AL,5    ;set write mode
            mov     AH,2    ;mode 2 (color n to masked bits)
            word_out

            endm

plot        macro

;Assumes page is 0, but similar to INT 10 in other respects:
;AL = color
;CX = column
;DX = row

            push    BX
            push    CX
            push    DX
            push    AX          ;done last for use near end

            push    DX

            mov     AX,CX   ;put the column number in AX
            push    CX          ;save the column number
            mov     CL,16-pixpb         ;find AX mod pixels per
                                        ; byte through shifts
            shl     AX,CL
            shr     AX,CL
            mov     CL,AL
            mov     AL,b_mask           ;create a bit mask by
            shr     AL,CL   ;rotate the bit mask into place
            pop     CX      ;restore CX

            mov     AH,AL   ;put the bit mask in AH
```

```
        mov     AL,8      ;bit mask register index
        mov     DX,3ceh   ;bit mask register
        word_out

        pop     DX

        mov     AX,DX             ;put the row in AX
        mov     BX,bprow          ;get bytes per row
        mul     BX                ;multiply by bytes/row
        mov     BX,CX             ;put column number in BX
        mov     CL,pixpb

        shr     BX,CL             ;divide by pixels / byte
        add     BX,AX             ;byte offset in memory

        mov     AX,ega_mem
        mov     ES,AX
        mov     AL,ES:[BX]        ;load the latch registers
        pop     AX                ;restore the color number
        mov     ES:[BX],AL        ;write color to memory

        pop     DX
        pop     CX
        pop     BX

        endm

; END OF MACROS — THE FOLLOWING CODE
; DEMONSTRATES THE USE OF THE
; LINE MACROS

dgroup    group   data

data      segment public
          x_1     dw      150
          y_1     dw      175
          x_n     dw      320
          y_n     dw      5
          color   db      5

          o_mode  db      ?
          o_curs  dw      ?

data      ends

code      segment public
          assume  cs:code
```

```
main        proc    far

start:      push    DS
            sub     AX,AX
            push    AX

            mov     AX,dgroup
            mov     DS,AX

            assume  DS:dgroup

            mov     AH,0fh   ;get current mode information
            int     10h
            mov     o_mode,AL          ;save the current mode

            mov     AH,3     ;get the cursor attributes
            int     10h
            mov     o_curs,CX          ;save the cursor type

            mov     AX,10h   ;set mode to hi-res graphics
            int     10h

            line    x_1,y_1,x_n,y_n
            mov     y_n,345
            mov     color,2
            line    x_1,y_1,x_n,y_n

            mov     x_1,320
            mov     x_n,490
            mov     y_n,175
            mov     AX,1000
bmrk:
```

;this loop can be used for benchmarking variations in the code
;It also gives a good demonstration of the plotting speed by
;cycling through the colors

```
            mov     color,al
            and     color,1111b
            push    AX

            mov     y_1,5
            line    x_1,y_1,x_n,y_n,

            mov     y_1,345
            line    x_1,y_1,x_n,y_n
```

```
           pop    AX
           dec    AX
           jz     go_on
           jmp    bmrk
go_on:
           mov    AH,0     ;return mode to original value
           mov    AL,o_mode
           int    10h

           mov    AH,1     ;set cursor type
           mov    CX,o_curs        ;restore the cursor type

           int    10h

           ret

main       endp

code       ends

end        start
```

VERTIRQ2.ASM uses the hardware interrupt to write a line of V's across the top of the screen. A second line of V's is continuously written. The first line remains steady while the second flickers rapidly (the second line being drawn almost as fast as the computer will allow). Contrast this to VERTINT, which is similar, but can only write the second line after writing the first — thus slowing the execution of the main routine. A complete description of this process is given in Chapter 14.

Assembly Language Example:

```
clr_flg      equ     1
ecd_flg      equ     2
vga_flg      equ     4
vr_bit       equ     8
g64_flg      equ     16
cols         equ     50h

set_irq2     macro
             Local    chk_disp, chk_mem, chk_done, no_vga, vga,
                      skip_prm

;DS must be set to DATA when this macro is used

             push     DS

             mov      AX,BIOS
             mov      DS,AX    ;set the data segment to
                              ; the BIOS save area
             assume   DS:BIOS
             xor      AH,AH
             mov      AL,mode;get the current video mode

             pop      DS
             assume   DS:DATA

             test     hdwre,vga_flg
             jz       no_vga
             jmp      vga
no_vga:      cmp      AL,3
             jbe      chk_disp
             cmp      AL,0fh
             jae      chk_mem
             jmp      chk_done

chk_disp:
             test     hdwre,ecd_flg         ;is the color alpha
```

```
                                          ; mode set to 350 lines?
            jz      chk_done              ; no, use the standard
                                          ; parameter table entry
            add     AX,19                 ;350 line alpha requires
                                          ; the mode+19 entry in
                                          ; the parameter table
            jmp     chk_done

chk_mem:
            test    hdwre,g64_flg         ;is more than 64K memory
                                          ; installed on the EGA?
            jz      chk_done              ; no, use the standard

                                          ; parameter table entry
            add     AX,2                  ;>64K, 350 line graphics
                                          ; requires the mode+2
                                          ; entry in the
                                          ; parameter table
            jmp     chk_done

vga:        mov     DX,CRT_add            ;the VGA can read the
                                          ; current V. Ret. End
            mov     AL,11h   ;index of Vertical Retrace End
            out     DX,AL
            inc     DX
            in      AL,DX    ;get the current value
            mov     AH,AL    ;put the current setting in AH
                                          ; for later use
            jmp     skip_prm

chk_done:
            push    DS

            lds     BX,prm_tbl
            assume  DS:nothing
            mov     CL,6
            shl     AX,CL    ;multiply AX by bytes per mode
            add     AX,27    ;add offset of
                                          ; Vertical Retrace End entry
            add     BX,AX    ;BX is now memory offset of
                                          ; desired entry

            mov     AH,[BX]
            pop     DS
            assume  DS:data

skip_prm:   and     AH,11001111b          ;enable and clear IRQ2
```

```
                                    ; (other bits unchanged)

            mov     DX,CRT_add
            mov     AL,11h
            out     DX,AL
            inc     DX
            mov     AL,AH   ;put the IRQ2 settings in AL
            out     DX,AL
            or      AL,10000b          ;finish enabling IRQ2
            out     DX,AL

            endm

BIOS        segment at 40h

            org     49h
mode        db      ?

            org 0a8h
save_wptr           label       word
save_ptr dd         ?

BIOS        ends

stack       segment stack

            db      100 dup ('stack  ')

stack       ends

data        segment public

even
            wrd_i0a label       word
            old_i0a dd          ?
            prm_wtbl            label       word
            prm_tbl dd          ?

            CRT_add             dw      3b4h    ;default CRT address
                                                ; register (monochrome)

            hdwre   db      0           ;hardware flags (color
                                        ; monitor, ecd, etc)
            int_st  db      ?           ;programmable interrupt
                                        ; controller mask
data        ends
```

```
code        segment public
            assume CS:code

            main proc far

start:
            push DS
            sub     AX,AX
            push    AX

            mov     AX,data
            mov     DS,AX
            assume  DS:data

            mov     AX,BIOS
            mov     ES,AX
            assume  ES:BIOS

            les     BX,ES:save_ptr      ;load ES:BX with the
                                        ;address of the SAVE_PTR

            assume  ES:nothing
            les     BX,ES:[bx]          ;load ES:BX with the
                                        ;address of the parameter
                                        ;table (first entry in
                                        ;the SAVE_PTR table)

            mov     prm_wtbl,BX
            mov     prm_wtbl[2],ES

            mov     BL,10h  ;get EGA information
            mov     AH,12h  ;alternate functions
            int     10h     ;BIOS call

            cmp     BL,0    ;Is more than 64K installed
            jz      lt64k   ;no, do not set g64_flg
            or      hdwre,g64_flg

lt64k:
            cmp     BH,1    ;Is it a monochrome
            je      mono    ;yes, defaults already set for
                            ;monochrome, skip setup

            cmp     CL,1001b            ;Check switch settings.
                                        ;Is it an enhanced display?
            je      ecd
            cmp     CL,0011b            ; in hi-res alpha mode
            je      ecd
```

```
            jmp     cd          ;no, it is a normal color display
                                ;(or ECD in emulation mode)

ecd:        or      hdwre,ecd_flg

cd:         or      hdwre,clr_flg
            mov     CRT_add,3d4h

mono:
            mov     AX,1a00h                ;read display combination
            int     10h         ;BIOS video call

            cmp     AL,1ah      ;the VGA (or 30) will return 1ah
            jne     not_vga

            cmp     BL,7        ;is it a monochrome VGA?
            je      yes_vga
            cmp     BL,8        ;is it a color VGA?
            je      yes_vga
            jmp     not_vga

yes_vga:    or      hdwre,vga_flg

not_vga:    mov     AX,350ah                ;put the current INT 0ah
                                            ;address in ES:BX
            int     21h         ;DOS function call

            mov     wrd_i0a,bx
            mov     wrd_i0a[2],es

            test    hdwre,vga_flg
            jz      do_test
            jmp     skip_test;no need to test retrace
                        ; polarity on VGA

do_test:
            push    DS

            mov     AX,CS
            mov     DS,AX       ;set DS same as CS in order to set
                                ;the interrupt vector
            mov     DX,offset fake_i0a ;this is the retrace bit
                                        ;polarity test
            mov     AX,250ah                ;change int 0ah to address
                                            ;in DS:DX
            int     21h         ;DOS function call
```

```
          pop     DS

          set_irq2

          push    AX          ;save interrupt value

          in      AL,21h   ;get the interrupt controller status
          mov     int_st,AL               ;save the interrupt controller
                                          ;status
          and     AL,11111011b   ;make sure IRQ2 is
                                 ;enabled (set to 0)
          out     21h,AL

          mov     DX,CRT_add
          mov     AL,11h
          out     DX,AL
          pop     AX                      ;restore interrupt value

          or      AL,100000b     ;disable IRQ2
                                 ;(force interrupt)
          inc     DX
          out     DX,AL

skip_test:
          push    DS

          mov     AX,CS
          mov     DS,AX    ;set DS same as CS in order to set
                          ;the interrupt vector
          mov     DX,offset new_i0a

          mov     AX,250ah            ;change int 0ah to address
                                      ;in DS:DX
          int     21h      ;DOS function call

          pop     DS

          set_irq2

          mov     CX,3
hold2:    push    CX
          mov     CX,2000h
          mov     AX,0b800h
          test    hdwre,clr_flg
          jnz     seg_ok
          sub     AX,800h
seg_ok:   mov     ES,AX
```

```
hold:       push    CX
            mov     CX,Cols  ;number of columns to write
            mov     DI,0a0h  ;starting at byte 0a0h
            mov     AX,0720h            ;write blanks, attribute 7
            rep     stosw
            mov     CX,Cols
            mov     DI,0a0h
            mov     AX,0756h            ;write the letter "V",
                                        ;attribute 7

            rep     stosw
            pop     CX

            loop    hold
            pop     CX
            loop    hold2

            mov     AL,int_st           ;restore the interrupt
                                        ;controller status
            out     21h,AL

            mov     AH,0fh  ;get current video mode
            int     10h

            and     AX,007fh            ;clear high bit of AL and
                                        ;set AH to 0
            int     10h     ;set mode (this will
                                        ;clear the IRQ2)

            lds     DX,old_i0a
            assume  DS:nothing
            mov     AX,250ah            ;restore int 0ah to its original
                                        ;address (in DS:DX)
            int     21h     ;DOS function call

            mov     AH,0fh  ;get current video mode
            int     10h

            and     AX,007fh            ;clear high bit of AL and
                                        ;set AH to 0
            int     10h     ;set mode (this will
                                        ;clear the IRQ2)

            ret
```

```
new_i0a      proc     far

             cli                 ;disable interrupts
             push     AX
             push     DX
             push     DI
             push     DS
             push     ES

             mov      AX,data
             mov      DS,AX
             assume   DS:data

             mov      DX,3c2h  ;was IRQ2 from the EGA?
                               ;(Input Status Register Zero)
             in       AL,DX
             test     AL,80h   ;mask off the vertical
                               ;interrupt bit
             jnz      cnt_vr
             jmp      skp_vr

cnt_vr:      mov      AX,0b800h           ;starting address for
                               ;color alpha display
             test     hdwre,clr_flg
             jnz      seg_ok2
             sub      AX,800h  ;starting address for
                               ;mono alpha display
seg_ok2:     mov      ES,AX

             push     CX
             mov      CX,Cols  ;number columns to fill
             mov      DI,0     ;starting at byte 0a0h
             mov      AX,0720h            ;write blanks, attribute 7
             rep      stosw
             mov      CX,Cols
             mov      DI,0
             mov      AX,0756h            ;write the letter "V",
                               ;attribute 7
             rep      stosw
             push     BX
             set_irq2            ;clear current IRQ2
             pop      BX
             pop      CX

skp_vr:
             pushf               ;required to simulate INT
             call     [old_i0a]
```

```
        pop     ES
        pop     DS
        pop     DI
        pop     DX
        pop     AX

        iret
```

;this routine assumes the old INT 0ah routine send an
; End of Interrupt (EOI)
;BIOS originally points to an EOI routine, and all other
; interrupt handlers should either use the BIOS routine or
; one of their own
;It also assumes the routine contains the required IRET
; instruction

```
new_i0a    endp

fake_i0a   proc    far

           cli                     ;disable interrupts

           push    AX
           push    DX
           push    DI
           push    DS
           push    ES

           mov     AX,data
           mov     DS,AX
           assume  DS:data

           mov     DX,3c2h ;get IRQ2 status
                           ;(Input Status Register Zero)
           in      AL,DX
           test    AL,80h  ;mask off the vertical
                           ;interrupt bit
           jnz     nrm_vr  ;the bit is set
                           ;(standard EGA method)

           or      hdwre,vr_bit    ;the vertical retrace
                                   ;bit is reversed

nrm_vr:

           set_irq2        ;clear current IRQ2
```

```
        pushf                ;required to simulate INT
        call     [old_i0a]

        pop      ES
        pop      DS
        pop      DI
        pop      DX
        pop      AX

        iret
```

;This routine assumes the old INT 0ah routine send an
; End of Interrupt (EOI)
;BIOS originally points to an EOI routine, and all other
; interrupt handlers should either use the BIOS routine
; or one of their own
;It also assumes the routine contains the required IRET
; instruction

```
fake_i0a    endp

main        endp

code        ends

end         start
```

VERTINT.ASM polls the vertical retrace status bit, and writes a line of V's across the top of the screen when the retrace is detected. A second line of V's is written in the main body of the program. While the main body does not check for a vertical retrace, it may only proceed after the subroutine which writes the first line. Thus, the second line will also print during the retrace. Contrast this to VER-TIRQ2, which is similar, but can write the second line as fast as the CPU will allow. VERTIRQ2's two writing routines are essentially independent, and the second line flickers.

Assembly Language Example:

```
clr_flg      equ      1

stack        segment stack

             db       100 dup ('stack   ')

stack        ends

data         segment public

even

             ST_add  dw      3bah
                              ;default Status Register 1
                              ; address (monochrome)

             hdwre   db       0
                              ;hardware flags
                              ; (color monitor, ecd)

data         ends

code         segment public
             assume CS:code

             main proc far

start:

             push DS
             sub      AX,AX
             push     AX

             mov      AX,data
             mov      DS,AX
             assume   DS:data
```

```
                mov      BL,10h    ;get EGA information
                mov      AH,12h    ;alternate functions
                int      10h       ;BIOS call

lt64k:
                cmp      BH,1      ;Is it a monochrome
                je       mono      ;yes, defaults already set
                                   ; for monochrome, skip setup

                or       hdwre,clr_flg
                mov      ST_add,3dah


mono:
                mov      CX,400h

                mov      AX,0b800h
                test     hdwre,clr_flg
                jnz      seg_ok
                sub      AX,800h
seg_ok:         mov      ES,AX

hold:           push     CX
                mov      CX,50h
                mov      DI,0a0h
                mov      AX,0720h
                rep      stosw
                mov      CX,50h
                mov      DI,0a0h
                mov      AX,0756h
                rep      stosw
                pop      CX

                call     int_v

                loop     hold

                ret

int_v           proc     near

                push     AX
                push     BX
                push     CX
                push     DX
                push     DI
                push     DS
```

```
            push    ES

            mov     AX,data
            mov     DS,AX
            assume  DS:data

no_rt:      mov     DX,ST_add           ;Status Register One
            in      AL,DX   ;test the vertical retrace status bit
            test    AL,1000b            ;is it in a vertical retrace?
            jnz     no_rt   ; yes, keep looking for
                            ; non-retrace (display) interval

n_rt:       in      AL,DX   ;now, it is displaying so we
                            ; can check for the beginning

            test    AL,1000b            ; of the vertical retrace. Is it
                            ; in a vertical retrace?
            jz      n_rt    ; no, try again.

            mov     AX,0b800h           ;starting address for
                            ; color alpha display

            test    hdwre,clr_flg
            jnz     seg_ok2
            sub     AX,800h ;starting address for
                            ; mono alpha display
seg_ok2:    mov     ES,AX
            mov     DI,0
            mov     CX,50h
            mov     AX,0720h
            rep     stosw
            mov     CX,50h
            mov     DI,0
            mov     AX,0756h
            rep     stosw

            pop     ES
            pop     DS
            pop     DI
            pop     DX
            pop     CX
            pop     BX
            pop     AX

            ret

int_v       endp
```

```
main        endp

code        ends

end         start
```

Index

Save time by ordering a source code diskette.

All of the source code from *EGA/VGA: A Programmer's Reference Guide* is available on a 5-1/4-inch diskette. Each assembly language program has been assembled to an .EXE file, so a micro assembler is not necessary.

To order, send $21.00 plus $4.00 shipping and handling. Indiana residents add 5% sales tax. Illinois, Michigan, Minnesota, Ohio, and Wisconsin residents should also add applicable sales tax. Please do not send cash. Check, Money Order, VISA, and MasterCard accepted.

DK Micro Consultants
816 Auto Mall Road
Dept. 222
Bloomington, IN 47401

or call (812) 333-1518

If ordering by credit card please provide:

Name (as on card): _____
MasterCard # (16 digits): _____
or VISA # (13 or 16 digits): _____
Expiration Date: _____

Cardholder's signature: _____

DATE DUE

7/30/90			
8/20/90			
SEP 0 3 1990			
6-14-91			
MAR 2 9 1993			
JAN 0 5 1994			
GAYLORD			PRINTED IN U.S.A.